Great Hunters

Their trophy rooms & collections

Safari Press Inc.

P. O. Box 3095, Long Beach, CA 90803

First edition

Safari Press Inc.

1998, Long Beach, California

ISBN 1-57157-111-6

Library of Congress Catalog Card Number: 97-67705

10 9 8 7 6 5 4 3 2 1

Readers wishing to receive the Safari Press catalog, featuring many fine books on big-game hunting, wingshooting, and sporting firearms, should write to Safari Press Inc., P.O. Box 3095, Long Beach, CA 90803, USA. Tel: (714) 894-9080, or visit our Web site at http://www.safaripress.com.

TABLE OF CONTENTS

INTRODUCTION

Trophy rooms are a hunter's memoirs of his adventures into the vast unpopulated portions of this wide, wild world in which we live—whether it be to the lofty peaks of the Pamirs of Russia, the Altai of Mongolia, the desert of Chad, or the rain forest of the Central African Republic. Each animal displayed represents a memory—a memory of sacrifice, triumph, personal achievement, humor, honor, or pathos. Each magnificent trophy has its own tale to tell.

There are many reasons a hunter chooses to hunt, and it certainly is not just to shoot an animal. The hunt is composed of myriad experiences that shape the person and hunter, and is not reflected in the single act of pulling the trigger of a gun or letting an arrow fly. The hunt encompasses the travel—whether to foreign or domestic locations—the interaction with the native population, the enlightenment of learning about new cultures and ideas, the shared camaraderie of the people with which they hunt, the understanding of the habits and habitats of the animals of the area, the history of a hunting location, and so on.

Hunters are lucky in that they have the opportunity to venture into unfamiliar countries where they often encounter historically significant artifacts and architectural achievements. Firsthand, they are there to appreciate the enduring nature of these monuments and structures, and they can see for themselves how these ancient civilizations, many thousands of years old, have helped to shape our understanding of our world. I, personally, recall the time when I was hunting ibex within the ancient city walls of a long-forgotten Roman city. Surrounded and awe-struck by my environment, I could have easily laid my rifle down and just become a tourist.

A responsible hunter is an educator. It is the hunter's responsibility to teach others about his role in the conservation of wildlife. In most cases, a hunter's trophy room is not only a showcase, but also a classroom that can be used as a tool for the education of people who do not hunt.

Hunters should let others know that as a conservationist, it is the hunter who contributes monetarily to the support of wildlife and to the protection of nature's habitats that is mandatory for the survival of wildlife. By continued attendance and involvement in endeavors for wildlife preservation, such as the Safari Club International's annual convention, hunters can become instrumental in achieving governmental and educational support for conservation programs. Without the world presence of Safari Club International, our hunting heritage would be greatly reduced, instead of appreciated and preserved. As you read through this book, you will see the trophy rooms of great hunters who have taken considerable care to preserve and showcase their hunting achievements. These hunters also generously give of their financial resources and commit their energies to conserve wildlife.

We, the hunters of the world, want to leave our children and grandchildren the legacy of this tremendous sport. Though we are competitive sportsmen, we want to help those fellow hunters who follow in our footsteps. We must endeavor to leave a clean, precise trail for them to follow, by obeying all the game laws of the countries we visit, as well as all the rules within our own country. As hunters we are, and must be, the sentinels of the fauna and flora of the world.

Warren K. Parker
Past President,
Safari Club International

The photos here and on the title page depict eminent hunters and their trophies, circa 1914. Luminaries of the day include W. N. McMillan, J. E. R. Oldfield, and Lord Wenlock of Great Britain.

BRITISH SPORTS & SPORTSMEN 1914

HIMMELSEHER

At the age of 80, I can make the happy statement that my hunting ambitions have resulted in keeping me physically fit and in top form. It has been my desire for first-class trophies from the very beginning, and I have made it a priority during my hunting career to seek out the oldest, the most mature of any species. However, for as long as I had my own hunting area in Germany, the preservation and care of it superseded any other desire.

For me, memories of the hunt are a paradise, a place that is always welcoming. I have hunted throughout all five continents, and consequently, my paradise is very large indeed! Until now I have submitted over 360 trophies to the Safari Club International for entry in the record books; 302 of these trophies have been considered, and 63 of them are among the top ten. In addition, I have acquired twenty-nine Grand Slams, five Africa Big Five Awards, seven Great Cats of the World awards, and four Bears of the World trophies.

For me, the finest days of my life were those that I spent hunting, and, God willing, there will be many more of them in the future!

MADDOX
(1909-1998)

Born in Easonville, Alabama, on 9 June 1909, Dan Maddox started in the finance industry after graduating from Georgia Tech in 1929, and he continued his activities in finance until his death. From 1930 until WW II, Mr. Maddox served as regional manager for the southeast for CIT Corporation, a pioneer in automobile finance.

Mr. Maddox served on the boards of numerous companies as well as many charitable and civic boards. He was listed in Who's Who in America, and Who's Who in the South and Southeast since 1975.

Mr. Maddox had an intense interest in the wildlife of the world. He served for a number of years as a trustee for the African Wildlife Leadership Foundation. He was a past president and director of the Shikar Safari Club International. In 1973, Mr. Maddox cofounded the Shikar Safari Conservation Foundation, which now maintains worldwide activity in wildlife conservation. Mr. Maddox donated a very substantial collection of animals displayed in their natural habitats to the Lewis County Museum in Hohenwald, Tennessee.

In 1967, Mr. Maddox was awarded the Weatherby Big Game Trophy; he won the Winchester Award for the best Asian trophy and the Allwyn-Cooper Award for the best Indian trophy; and he was inducted into the Hunting Hall of Fame. Mr. Maddox received the Shikar Safari Conservation Award, and in 1996, he received the inaugural Dan Maddox Conservation Award from Quail Unlimited. In 1997, he was inducted into the Belmont University Collegiatus.

At the time of his death, Mr. Maddox operated an 850-acre farm in Tennessee, which he devoted exclusively to the propagation of deer, turkey, and quail. The following are Mr. Maddox's own words on his hunting, written before his death.

****

I have been a hunter all my life. I started hunting in Africa over forty years ago, sometimes accompanied by my wife, Margaret, and have, in all, made twenty-seven safaris in Africa, eight in Asia, and numerous hunts in North and South America to complete my trophy collections. I have collected the big five over three safaris and completed the Grand Slam of the Seven Spiral Horned Antelope—the bongo, greater kudu, lesser kudu, sitatunga, mountain nyala, plains nyala, and bushbuck. These seven trophies required six safaris, and took me all the way from Ethiopia to South Africa.

After this collection was completed, I hunted Africa's two browsing animals, the dibatag in Somalia, and the gerenuk in Uganda, as well as various types of the more common game: wildebeest, impala, Thompson and Grant gazelle, topi, sassaby, and hartebeest.

The wild sheep of the world have always fascinated me, for they live in the most remote and difficult to reach mountains. I was the third person to complete the Super Slam of Wild Sheep, which consists of fourteen or more species of this animal.

I have also completed a desert animal collection that includes the scimitar-horned oryx, addax, dama gazelle, and Barbary sheep. All were collected in the Sahara of northern Chad.

SPAULDING

Huck Spaulding was born 5 December 1928, in South Westerlo, a small farming community west of Albany, New York. Huck started his career in hunting and trapping when he was ten years old, largely due to the influence of his father who had a great interest in the outdoors and was always there to support and encourage him. In 1947, as a member of the 4-H Club of America, Huck competed in a 4-H fox-trapping program. He trapped 135 foxes, winning the six-week competition.

He later began tattooing as a hobby. By 1955, however, he was tattooing professionally, and today Spaulding & Rogers Manufacturing is the largest supplier of tattoo equipment in the world. Using his experience in tattooing, Spaulding was instrumental in implementing the Yellowstone National Park and New York State Bear Identification Program, which is a program that tattoos problem bears.

An avid hunter, Huck has hunted in sixty-two states and countries around the world and has gone on nineteen safaris to Africa. Huck has won numerous awards, including the World Congress Hunting Award (1988); the World Hunting Award SCI (1995); and the Hunter of the Year Award, SCI Tri-State (1996). He is also a founding sponsor of the International Wildlife Museum, Associates Program; a national SCI member, and an NRA lifetime member.

Huck's trophy room displays approximately 235 species, of which, as of 1995, 230 are in the record books, with 44 in the top ten. Huck Spaulding's trophy rooms were personally designed and crafted by Frank J. Zitz & Company.

His North American Room includes a large set of cliffs with the wild sheep of North America, a muskox in a snow scene cornered by two wolves, and a section of bears from North America and Russia including the #1 European brown bear. The room has a log cabin feel with yellow birch and alder foliage spreads, which give the year-round impression of a warm October afternoon.

The European Room includes a fine collection of red stags of the world, Asian deer, Baltic European boars, an antler chandelier, and European-style carved game-head panels.

Besides African fauna in the African Room, Huck has designed a forty-foot-wide set of cliffs to house his twenty sheep, ibex, chamois, and goats of the world. When you first walk in, there is a large rock cliff through which you enter into a lush Cameroon jungle diorama with life-size duikers, bongos, monkeys, a running waterfall, and a full forty-foot by twenty-foot wall of trophy African game heads. The rock cliffs in this trophy room start from a cool, blue winter scene and transform into a warm, red jungle scene for mood and atmosphere.

POCIUS

I was first introduced to hunting by my father and uncles when I was twelve. My earliest memories of hunting were those first days of the small game season in eastern Pennsylvania. My family would gather at our farm and conduct a hunt for pheasant, rabbit, and squirrel. At the end of the day, the game would be brought back to the farmhouse where my grandparents would clean and prepare it for a giant wild-game dinner. I can still remember sitting there listening to the tales of "the ones that got away,"—hanging on every word and experience, barely able to contain myself until the day I turned twelve and would be able to go hunting too.

By age fourteen, I loved the hunt so much that I also took up the bow, enabling me to extend my hunting time in the state. Today, I still take my bow almost everywhere I go, and, in Africa, I used it to take many animals, even a lion!

I've always been infatuated with the whitetail and its ability to adapt to environments all over the United States. I have been on over one hundred fifty whitetail hunts in the past thirty-nine years, and have taken over fifty whitetails that qualify for Pope & Young or Boone & Crockett. They are truly some of my greatest trophies. I have also hunted sheep for almost my entire career, and collected the Grand Slam of North America and the World Super Slam. In all, I've collected over eighteen species of wild sheep.

My love of hunting and adventure have taken me all over the world—to six continents where I've taken over 206 species—and I've collected many wonderful artifacts along the way: a Pygmy crossbow from the CAR and knives and swords from Ethiopia and the Sudan.

I also believe in "giving back" to nature, and so I joined Safari Club International in 1976, as well as various other professional hunting organizations. I became SCI's president in 1991, and I'm proud to say that under my direction we provided the seed money to start the Congressional Sportsman Caucus Foundation in Washington, D.C., which is now the largest sporting caucus in Washington. Through this foundation, SCI has been able to achieve considerable political victories over the years. I've also been fortunate enough to be the editor for the first World Bowhunting Record Book that SCI produced several years ago.

Although the awards and books and work I've done in the name of the hunt is extremely fulfilling to me, it is my trophy room that is dearest to my heart. It is a wonderful, life-size reflection of all the places I've been, the people I've met, and friends I've made all over the world—as well as a record of the challenges I have met and the rewards I have received. As I look around this room, I realize there hasn't been a place where I haven't made a friend or haven't enjoyed the experience. I feel truly blessed.

CAVERT

As a boy hunting small game in the hills of Tennessee in the 1930s, I developed what could be called an "impossible dream." I was driven by this dream—the dream of traveling the world and hunting big game. I envisioned tracking polar bears across the ice of the polar regions, stalking the big five through the grasses and thornbush of Africa, climbing the mountains of North America in search of the grand slam, wingshooting the bird-darkened skies of Central and South America, foot-trekking across Asia in pursuit of some of the world's greatest sheep, and slipping behind the Iron Curtain in Europe to hunt whatever they would let me hunt.

The Depression made this dream impossible, of course, so instead, I read everything about hunting I could get my hands on. From Sports Afield, I graduated to and devoured Hemingway, O'Connor, and most importantly, Roosevelt. Their detailed experiences of big-game hunting fueled, broadened, and became my desire.

Through time and by God's grace, my boyhood dreams became reality. In 1969, I made my first big-game hunt to Botswana. Since that time, I have made more than one hundred big-game hunts to many countries on most of the continents of the world: the United States, Alaska, Africa, Asia, Europe, Spain, Central America, Canada, Mexico, Australia, New Zealand, and the polar region at the 80th Parallel at the edge of the polar ice, north of Norway. I have hunted Africa eleven times, in such countries as Botswana, Tanzania, Zambia, Ethiopia, Zimbabwe, the Central African Republic, and the Republic of South Africa.

More than 100 of my 500 big-game trophies are world class. My collection includes the big five of Africa (elephant, lion, Cape buffalo, leopard, and black rhino) as well as most of the major species of Africa. I have taken the Grand Slam of North American Sheep (all of which are record class) and a number of species of Asian sheep and ibex. My sheep collection contains several world records including the world record mouflon (twice) from behind the Iron Curtain in Czechoslovakia. I have collected almost all of the species of Eastern Europe.

In 1979, I realized the pinnacle of achievement of my boyhood dream when I established the Tillman Cavert Wildlife Museum at my alma mater, Cumberland University in Lebanon, Tennessee. The museum contains a number of my trophies, many of which are life size. One of the most satisfying aspects of my hunting experiences is the realization that my trophies are housed and enjoyed, while fostering education in an institution that is less than thirty miles from the hills where I first dreamed of hunting the big game of the world.

If life consists of a series of experiences, then three things are worthwhile: anticipation, execution, and memories. In order for one to create worthwhile memories, one must work to make them happen and one must execute what one anticipates. Such efforts usually result in once-in-a-lifetime experiences of unforgettable memories and unbounded joys. For me, they are the realization of my "impossible dream."

TOUBY
(1916-1996)

Harry Touby was a "man's man" who excelled at everything he attempted. The two things that really defined him, however, were his passions for building (construction), and hunting.

After WW II Harry returned to his home in Miami, Florida. There, he became a leader in the construction industry. His energy and outspoken common sense earned him a reputation for honesty, integrity, and excellence, and he was considered by many to be the most all-round knowledgeable general contractor in Florida. Lawmakers and public officials sought his opinions in technical matters relating to the construction industry, including insurance, lien laws, and workers' compensation. He was also primarily responsible for the licensing of professional engineers, and received License #1 in recognition of his efforts.

Harry was as enthusiastic about hunting as he was about building. He began hunting deer, elk, and bear in Colorado, Wyoming, Alaska, and the Northwest Territories in the early 1960s, but his interests rapidly moved to more exotic game. Around 1965, Harry made his first safari to Africa, and subsequently returned for approximately seven more hunts. During the next twenty years he also hunted in India, Mongolia, Paraguay, and many other distant countries.

Harry was also extremely active in animal conservation and the Safari Club International, eventually becoming a vice president and a director. On the local level, Harry was active in the South Florida Chapter of Safari Club International, and served as its president.

He used his engineering abilities to sharpen his hunting skills: He handloaded his ammunition and built a "shooting tunnel" to test his loads, and used a special computer program to record the statistics of the handloads. His children called him "Dead Eye," and it was a nickname that was well deserved, for he was a skillful and accurate shot.

Harry regaled his family and friends with his hunting stories and pictures, and we children particularly enjoyed the tales of his hunt for the "rare and elusive bongo." (For several years Harry hunted futilely for a bongo until it became a family joke.) He finally shot a fine specimen that became a showpiece in his collection.

Harry was a generous man who shared his love of hunting by introducing many of his friends to its excitement. In 1981 I accompanied my father on a hunt on horseback in Spain for red stag and mouflon. It was a memorable experience and broke his long-standing rule regarding hunting with women.

When Harry retired, he donated the bulk of his trophies to the World Wildlife Museum in Stockton, California. However, some of the family selected an animal as a memento. I chose a leopard for that hunt was one of his most challenging. He had to lie perfectly still and quiet for many hours on a machan, and the idea of my boisterous, energetic father remaining so still for so long has always fascinated me.

THUMMLER

Hubert Thummler has been a sportsman all his life. Learning to ride horses kept by his parents and grandparents in Germany, and later Mexico City, Thummler began jumping horses for shows at an early age. Later, he belonged to the juvenile Olympic team representing Mexico in several international events.

During his college years in the United States (Wisconsin and Missouri), he got the bug for fishing and hunting, but hunting is such an expensive sport that it took some years of building a business before he could support this hobby. Once he graduated from college, he went from horse jumping to motorcycle racing, and later, with his Porsche, became Mexico's Rally Champion in 1959, together with his copilot wife, Kitty.

Thummler was still determined to try his hand at hunting, and in 1971 he felt it was time to head for the wilderness to fulfill his dream of becoming an award-winning hunter. His first big-game hunt was in Baja California, for the cimarrón (Ovis canadensis nelsoni), the terminology for the desert sheep in Mexico. This was a great experience, and from then on he became obsessed with the hunt.

In those early years he had little knowledge on how to structure or sustain a hunting career because organizations like Safari Club International (SCI) did not exist. SCI was just beginning, and there were no record books, no statistics, and no lists with the names of the game to be hunted as well as no indication of where in the world to hunt the various game animals.

He joined SCI and began establishing connections with other hunters at conventions, but it was not until 1976 that Mr. Thummler met a very knowledgeable man in Mongolia who shared the camp with him. This man explained to Thummler the way to pursue fame in the hunting world. It was Dr. Jim Conklin, who soon after would receive the world's most prestigious hunting award, the Weatherby Trophy. The advice he gave was: "Go and collect all the trophy species of the world!"

Mr. Thummler has hunted on all continents, and has collected a total of 287 different trophy species, but he is especially proud of the 106 trophies he has taken from Africa and his 27 sheep trophies taken from various parts of the world (7 argalis, 5 urials, 11 ibexes, and 7 chamois). These trophies are a result of one hundred big-game hunts around the world in thirty-nine different countries.

After having obtained such an impressive collection, Thummler received the renowned Weatherby Award in 1992, and in 1993 the SCI International Hunting Award.

His trophy collection is in Tequisquapan, in the state of Querétaro, and will be donated to a museum in that city; the proceeds will go to a clinic for mentally and physically disabled children.

Mr. Thummler feels indebted to God for creating such a beautiful world, and to the professional hunters, trackers, cooks, and other help who enabled him to achieve his dream.

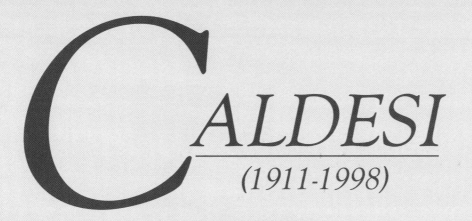

CALDESI
(1911-1998)

I was born in Milan, Italy, on 25 July 1911, and I was twelve when my father put a double-barreled shotgun in my hands for the first time. Pointing at the birds crossing overhead, he said, "It's time for you to start shooting. Try to drop one of them." I had never shot before, but I shot three times and did not miss once. Some months later he took me to a pigeon-shooting contest; with fifteen cartridges I shot fifteen targets and won the first prize. Thus my hunting career began, seventy-four years ago.

My father was an excellent shot and a hunter of great instinct, and I followed him with enthusiasm every time I could. When I grew up, I became a member of the Italian shooting team, and in 1956 I won the Monte Carlo Grand Prix, which, at that time, was the ultimate triumph for a dove shooter.

When I was forty-five, I was invited to Austria to shoot roe deer. I was given a 6.5x57 Mannlicher, with all the related hunting equipment. I immediately found it quite easy to shoot with a telescopic sight, and so my career as a big-game hunter began.

For my first safari in Kenya, I was lucky enough to get Fred Bartlett as my PH; my wife, Mara, accompanied me. I was immediately charmed by the hunts, the animals, and the scenery. I shot a black rhino that is still No. 1 in the SCI record book, and later that month I shot two elephants, one lion, two leopards, four buffaloes, and some thirty other animals of about twenty varieties. Those were the most glorious days of my life!

I returned to Africa many times, hunting those regions that offered me the opportunity to get new trophies, and I alternated safaris with shikars in India and with numerous expeditions to Nepal, Mongolia, Australia, and New Zealand. I also visited those parts of Asiatic Russia that were open. In addition, I have taken more than thirty hunts in America, mainly in Alaska and Canada. When I was in Europe, I was continually moving from one country to another and assiduously devoting myself to the hunt of ungulates; I also shot grouse in Central Europe.

I have taken over 250 hunts in forty-eight countries on six continents. I have collected 236 species of animals, over half of which are in the SCI record book. I was a founding member and first president of the SCI Italian chapter, and I am a member of the International Council for Game and Wildlife Conservation. I won the Weatherby Award in 1981; was admitted to the SCI Hunting Hall of Fame in 1983; became the Italian and European wingshooting champion several times; and in 1987 won the C. J. McElroy Award from SCI (name changed in 1998 to "International Hunting Award"), which honors excellence in hunting.

No matter where my hunting has taken me, I have always looked for animals that I had not yet acquired, or for some trophy more valuable than the ones I already owned. Several times I have come back from a long hunt without shooting, but I was never sorry to come home empty-handed because that meant I had stuck to the principles and ethics of sport hunting.

WHITEHEAD

Born in 1913 in Bury, Lancashire, Kenneth Whitehead always had an interest in natural history subjects, and during his youth devoted his attention to collecting bird's eggs, butterflies, and moths, as well as photographing birds.

Kenneth's interest in deer dates back to 1930 when he was staying with his uncle, S. D. Whitehead, for grouse shooting on the Mull of Kintyre, Scotland. One day they saw a sika, and he asked whether he could shoot one. His uncle kindly replied, "Certainly, and I'll arrange for you to go out with the keeper before your holiday ends." Two days later Kenneth shot an 8-point sika stag, and from then on, his interest in deer developed, and he took every opportunity to photograph and stalk the various species of deer around the world.

It was not until after his service as a major in the Royal Artillery during WW II that he began the Whitehead Museum. From 1950 onward, he undertook the monumental task of collecting under one roof many of the fine trophies that had been shot by earlier sportsmen during the late nineteenth and early twentieth centuries, which were being disposed of as large estates were sold.

Among the early acquisitions were trophies from the Sir E. Loder and J. G. Millais collections that included a big wapiti (elk) shot by J. G. Millais in Wyoming in 1886, and which is currently listed No. 7 in the Boone & Crockett record book (1993).

The Whitehead Museum is quite possibly the only private museum to house representatives of all the deer species in the world (forty different species—not including all the subspecies). The Whitehead Museum has complete skeletons (the majority of which were formerly in the Loder collection) of the extinct giant deer, Megaceros giganteus, the European bison, Rocky Mountain goat, Barbary sheep, blackbuck, gerenuk, muntjac, and miscellaneous antelope.

The Whitehead Museum is a private museum that can be viewed only by appointment. The museum, which is separate from Whitehead's house, was formerly an old coach house, consisting of stables and living quarters for the employees. It was built about a century and a half ago and has a total floor area of around 3,900 square feet. The museum consists of eight rooms.

Though he has no obvious favorite species of deer, Whitehead feels that the roe deer, Capreolus, is probably the most desirable trophy, for it is a deer that can be best hunted by a single stalker, and when shot, the carcass can be handled without assistance.

Apart from his regular stalking in England and Scotland, Whitehead's hunting trips abroad have included the U.S. (Montana, Texas), Canada (British Columbia), Europe (Belgium, Bulgaria, Czechoslovakia, France, Germany, Hungary, Italy, Norway, Romania, Sardinia, Spain, Sweden, and Yugoslavia), Iran, Australia, New Zealand, Africa, West Africa (Ghana, Nigeria), and South Africa. Trophies of various species that are representative of each country listed are included in the museum.

Kenneth Whitehead has written numerous articles in the sporting press, and is the author of fifteen books, most of which are about deer.

MALLOY

In 1945, twelve-year-old John J. "Jack" Malloy was sent to live on a small, northeastern Pennsylvania farm after the death of his parents. Along with him, Jack brought his dad's Marlin Model 39A .22 caliber rifle, a Winchester 94 .30-30 caliber, and a Fox double-barrel .12-gauge shotgun, and soon he became a keen hunter, supplying plenty of woodchucks, rabbits, and deer for the farmhouse dinner table. These first trophies are gone, but the guns still hang in Jack's gun rack today, well worn and well loved.

As Jack grew, so did his passion for the hunt. It was an easy transition from hunting in the mountains of the Catskills and Adirondacks to hunting in the rest of North America and around the world. When Jack was thirty, he had hunted moose, caribou, and bear in Canada and Newfoundland, and red deer in the Highlands of Scotland, and roe deer in the forests of Sussex.

In 1970, while still in Europe, Jack met Paul Roberts, a young hunter whose father owned a gun shop in the west end of London. Paul had just returned from his first trip to Africa, and the game trophies and elephant tusks he brought back ignited Jack's passion to hunt Africa. He purchased Hunter by J. A. Hunter, which became his bible, and a Jeffries .475 #2 double, a Winchester Model 70 .375 H&H, a Remington Model 700, a 7 Remington Magnum, and a Model 21 Winchester .12-gauge shotgun, which became his tools. With these and a prayer, his African adventure started.

In July 1972, Jack teamed up with his good friend Norman Flayderman for their first safari to Africa: a thirty-day hunt in the Selous Reserve in Tanzania. They hired guides, and from start to finish, the safari was magnificent, with each of them taking seventeen heads of plains game as well as elephant, lion, leopard, and hippo. After that, Jack was hooked for life.

Twenty-seven years later with twenty-five safaris to Africa, some over sixty days in length, he still hunts the "Burning Shores." Men like Tim and Luke Samaras, Tony Henley, Lionel Palmer, Terry Irwin, Alan Lowe, Fritz Mayer, and Jean Vannier were his friends and guides. From Ethiopia west to the Cameroons, and back south to Kenya, Tanzania, Botswana, and through South Africa, the safaris went on. And even though Jack has been on other hunts to Russia, Kyrgyzstan, Mongolia, India, Sweden, France, Poland, Germany, Austria, Spain, New Zealand, Australia, Canada, and the U.S., Africa remains his real passion.

Fifty-four years after his first hunt on the Pennsylvania farm, Jack still plans many trips to faraway lands, intent on pursuing his love of the hunt. He is a member of SCI, and greatly enjoys exchanging hunting tales with his fellow members. His sage advice to friends: "Hunt now, while you can, for you will be a long time in a pine box."

DREESZEN

As a native Montanan, big-game hunting has always been a significant part of my lifestyle. I was fortunate to grow up and live in a state that provided numerous hunting opportunities—as many as eleven big-game species at one time! Presently, there are nine huntable big-game species in the Big Sky Country of Montana.

My family always hunted. Every fall we looked forward to putting a couple of deer or antelope in the freezer, and maybe getting a set of horns to hang in my bedroom. When I was about ten years old, I got my first taste of big-game trophy hunting when I accompanied my father on a hunt—he shot a decent 5x5 mule deer buck near our home. The antlers were nowhere close to record-book size, but to a kid they were from the biggest buck in Montana. I was hooked from that moment on.

My first exposure to a real trophy room was in my teens when I worked for a neighbor, Old Ralph. He was a hunter and trapper, and had built an addition on to his home, which he had filled with many trophies he had collected over the years. To this sixteen-year-old hunter who had only taken pronghorn antelope and mule deer, it was an impressive room.

My memories of that far-off day in Old Ralph's trophy room have led my wife, Patty, and me to open our doors to Boy Scouts and other youngsters. We enjoy the wide-eyed looks of the young people who tour our trophy room nowadays. It is our hope that by opening our doors we have passed on to these youngsters our feelings about conservation and the great sport of hunting.

It has been my pleasure to have Patty as my hunting partner, not only on many Montana hunts, but to places such as Canada and Mexico. Coming from a nonhunting background, she has been very successful in her own right, taking many trophies, including two bighorn sheep.

I don't think we are much different than other hunter/conservationists, no matter what walk of life. We feel that we must give something back since we have received so much from the great outdoors. Presently, Patty is a lead Hunter Education Instructor in our area and was formerly secretary-treasurer of the Montana chapter of Safari Club International. I have served as president of the Montana chapter of Safari Club International, and currently, I am president of the Montana chapter of the Foundation for North American Wild Sheep.

Our trophy room is a complete collection, and houses not only some of the splendid game we have pursued, but memories of the hunt as well: memories of hunting bighorns in the mountains of Montana at 11,000 feet; sitting on a stand hunting for white-tailed buck in temperatures of 30 degrees below zero; long, blistering walks in search of Shiras moose; aching backs and sore shoulders from backpacking out meat and trophy.

Memories only hunters understand. . . .

DE LAULA

Ihigo Moreno y de Arteaga, the twelfth Marqués de Laula, was born in Madrid, Spain, on 18 April 1934; he is the third son of the Conde de los Andes, Grandee of Spain. His thesis, "Trotsky in Spain," earned him a degree in history from Madrid University. In 1961, he married H.R.H. Princess Teresa de Borbón Dos Sicílias; they have seven children.

A keen sportsman since childhood, he began shooting feathered game at the age of ten. When he was eighteen and had finished school, family tradition dictated he could now use a rifle, and soon after, he shot a wild boar, his first big game.

Although the Marqués has spent his professional career in shipping, he loves all types of hunting: stalking with a rifle, shotgun shooting at driven game, or pig shooting from a horse. Apart from his native Spain, he has hunted extensively in many parts of the world. His favorite type of pursuit is stalking mountain game, and his collection of trophies includes every species of chamois and ibex, and most species of wild sheep.

The Marqués's concern for conservation is a large part of his hunting instinct, and he has tried to involved himself heavily in conservationist efforts. He has been the manager of seven Spanish game reserves in the following regions: Montes de Toledo, Madrid, Sierra de la Demanda, Sierra de Gredos, Beceite, Cordillera Cantabrica, and the Pyrenees.

The Marqués's list of accomplishments is immense: He has been a member of the Spanish Trophy Committee for twenty-two years and was its president for the last twelve years; he has also been president of the Spanish delegation for the International Council for Game and Wildlife Conservation (C.I.C.) for fourteen years and chairman of the SCI International Advisory Committee (1988). He holds the "Medalla al mérito en la caza" awarded by the Federation of Spanish Hunters, and was elected as "Personalité de l'Année" for Sport and Wildlife in 1987. He is an active member of the Caprini Group of the C.I.C. and is the president of the Club de Monteros—the oldest hunting club in Spain.

He organized the first World Hunting Congress in Madrid in 1984, and the Venatoria exhibitions in Madrid in 1996 and 1997. He was responsible for arranging the presentation of Spanish trophies and was a member of the panel of judges at the fairs in Budapest in 1971, Turin in 1972 and 1973, and Marseille in 1977.

He is a regular contributor to national newspapers and specialty magazines, and he is the author of the following books: Fórmulas oficiales de homologación de los trofeos de caza (Madrid 1987), Domingo a Domingo (Seville 1987), and Cacerías en España (Madrid 1997). He is secretary of the Círculo de Bibliofília Venatoria, a society that he was instrumental in founding and whose purpose is to publish books on hunting topics.

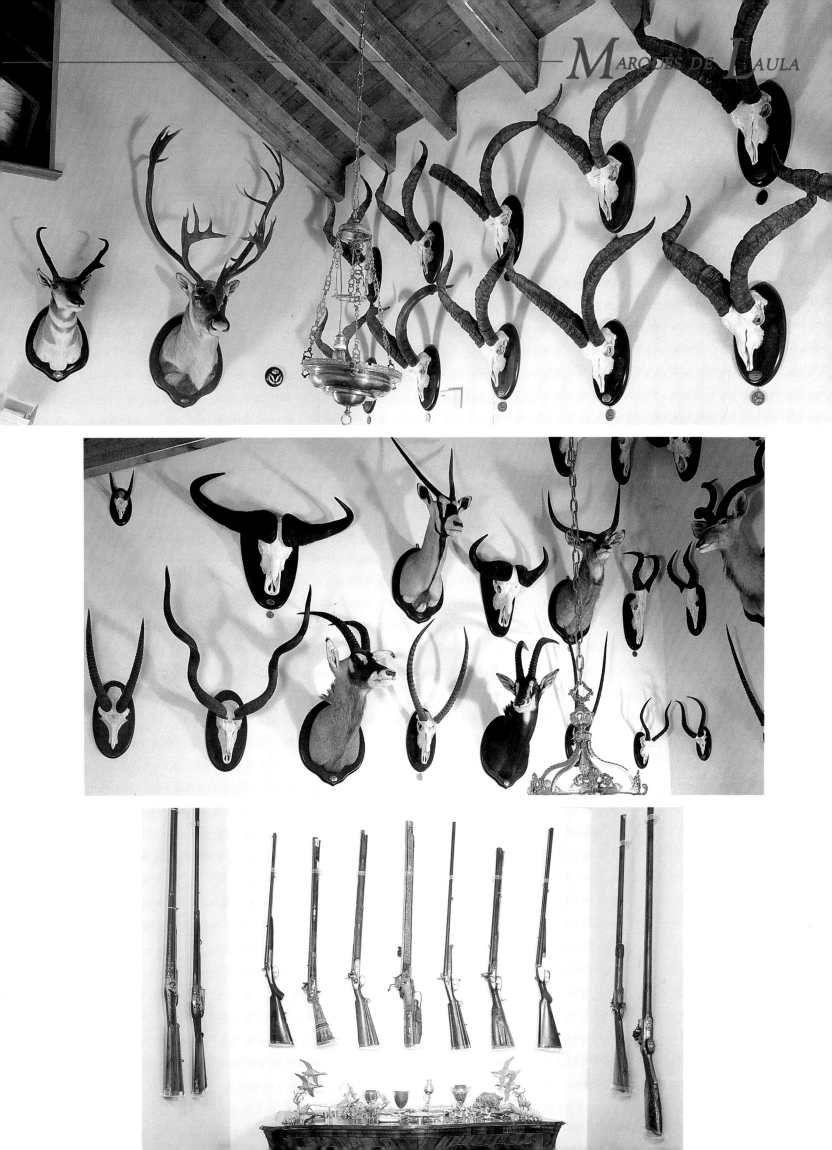

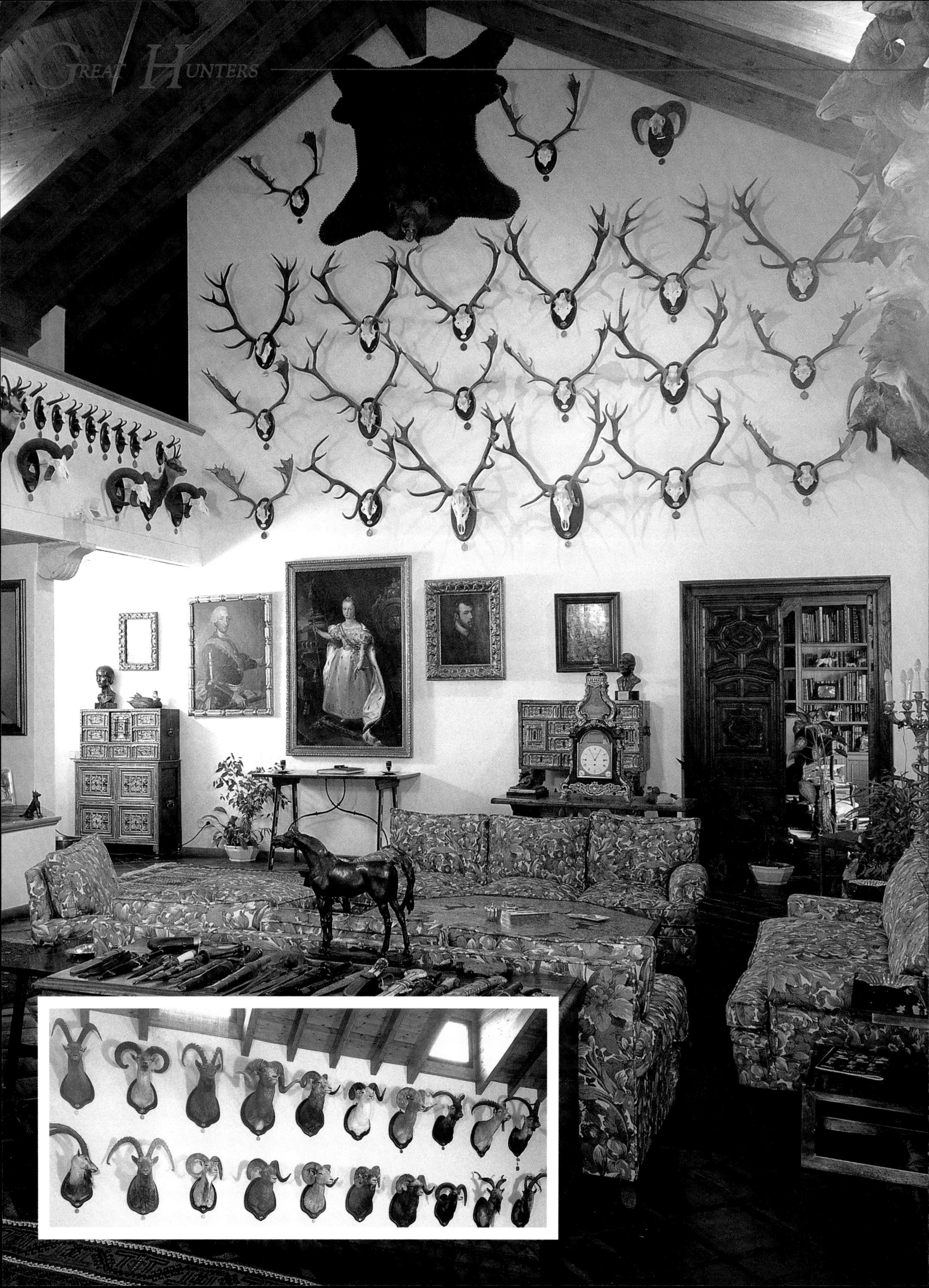

GUTIÉRREZ

A hunting trip with my father and brothers near our farm in Cuba in the late '50s is my first memory of a sport that I have increasingly come to enjoy over the years. The appreciation of nature and man's tradition of hunting are some things that have inspired me to experience the stalk in many places throughout the world.

In 1990, when designing a major addition to our home, my trophy room was conceived as a place of refuge from a busy and successful career as a geologist. It is in this room that I enjoy two of my greatest passions: the appreciation and collection of old double rifles and books on hunting in Africa and India. It is here where I reminisce on the adventures, the hunts, and the excitement of stalking many different types of game, especially in Africa. I spend many an evening relaxing in this room with a good book and, sometimes, a nice bottle of wine, while planning my next adventure. While the beauty of the mounts and how they complement the architecture of the room speaks for itself in the photographs, what I enjoy the most about my trophy room is being able to close my eyes and relive the stalk and the fellowship of the hunt, and share it with my family and friends.

While each type of hunting has its own unique appeal, if I had to choose a single animal to hunt, I would have to single out the elephant. The appreciation of the bush while carefully tracking a jumbo that could be one mile or ten miles away, and the anticipation of how you will approach and admire a beast as intelligent, as powerful, as majestic as an elephant is a part of the lure of this hunt. After having walked several hours from the Land Rover through the bush, listening and watching, I am transported to a time—maybe a hundred years ago—where schedules were dictated by the rhythms of the day and night, and when the days and the weeks and the months faded into one another. Suddenly, as if out of thin air, a six-ton beast emerges from behind the mopane trees, and immediately, all senses are focused on the approach, the observation, and the stalk. The intensity of this experience is unrivaled in our twenty-first-century world.

It is this appreciation for the hunting life and the bush that I share with my daughter in the way in which it was shared with me. The lure of Africa, the joy of a day well spent, and, perhaps the satisfaction of a successful hunt—it's good for the soul.

SCHRÖDER

For forty years, world-renowned hunter Consul General Manfred Schröder has represented the Republic of Ghana. During his many diplomatic journeys around the world and into nearly every corner of Africa, he has broadened his knowledge of local customs, gained a deeper understanding of the inhabitants, and undergone experiences quite beyond those encountered by the ordinary tourist. Herr Schröder also has received many invitations from kings, chiefs, and heads of state to join them in hunting expeditions.

Following a family tradition of hunting that goes back centuries, Consul General Schröder has collected trophies from forty years of hunting on every continent, which are housed in a private museum at his home in Germany. Herr Schröder has always followed important principles of game conservation, selecting his trophies from old or ill animals. He is a great follower of European hunting traditions, in keeping with his role as a knight grand officer in the Inter-national Order of St. Hubertus—a fraternal society of hunters established in 1695. His hunting prowess has led to his inclusion in the following record books: Rowland Ward, Boone and Crockett, and the Safari Club International.

His collection of trophies has been prepared both as full mounts and as wall-mounted heads by Klineburger Brothers in Seattle, Rowland Ward in London, Nico van Rooyen in Pretoria, and Zimmerman of Nairobi. The forms are fiberglass and each is accompanied by a CITES certificate. His collection is used for teaching natural science at schools and universities, and is recognized as one of the major mammal collections in the world.

As well as animals, his collection includes ethnographies and art gathered from all over the globe. Many of the carvings, drums, chairs, kente cloth, and metalwork were donated by monarchs, heads of state, and paramount chiefs.

His fauna and artifact collections are housed in a moated castle in Westphalia, Germany, which was built in 1595 as the seat of an abbess but is now owned by Mr. and Mrs. Schröder. The 1500-square-meter exhibit is open to the public and overseen by professional curators. The principle objective of the exhibit is to focus on the need for protection of the environment and endangered species. To that end Counsel General Schröder displays extinct mammals, threatened species, biotopes, varieties of timber, a collection of European and Mediterranean birds, and an exhibition of rural agricultural equipment of the nineteenth and early twentieth centuries.

In the park surrounding the castle, there are three elephants carved from granite that weigh some fifty tons, a totem pole eleven meters high, bronze casts of a red stag and doe, and a life-size group of wild boar carved from wood. The tower of a wooden church on the grounds contains three bells that are dedicated to St. Hubertus.

*K*ELLY

Larry Kelly, whose name has become synonymous with handgun hunting, founded the Handgun Hunters Hall of Fame in 1983. The museum displays well over one hundred of his personal trophies and is dedicated to furthering the American hunting heritage and to promoting the sport of handgun hunting. The museum is located in the 1200-square-foot, two-story lobby of Mag-na-port International, in Mt. Clemens, Michigan. It is the only trophy room in the world to display over 180 trophies taken by handgun only.

Over 135 medallion-emblazoned plaques from Safari Club International, signifying record-book animals, adorn the walls alongside the African big five, plains game, red stag, grizzly, moose, elk, and numerous North American trophies. A trophy room to satisfy even the most accomplished of big-game hunters, the hall houses the prestigious African Big Five Award from Safari Club International as well as plaques and letters of appreciation from numerous gun and hunting organizations. The Handgun Hunters Hall of Fame Museum is open to the public, and the facility is often made available to various sporting organizations, as well as the Cub and Boy Scouts.

Kelly, known for the invention of Mag-na-port (a unique recoil-taming process used on all types of firearms), had an unquenchable desire to hunt, especially with a handgun. He quickly became one of the world's most prominent handgun hunters, and he has opened doors for handgunners wishing to take many animals that have traditionally been taken with a rifle. His accomplishments in the advancement of handgunning have been recognized numerous times: In 1984 he received the Outstanding American Handgunner Award in honor of his lifetime pursuit of the sport of handgun hunting. In 1989, Larry Kelly was inducted into the Safari Club International Hunters Hall of Fame in recognition of his handgun hunting achievements. And, in 1995, the Michigan State Legislature passed a resolution honoring Larry Kelly for his lifelong efforts in the promotion of wildlife and preservation of the hunting heritage.

Kelly has hunted big game with a handgun for over forty-three years, taking seventy-seven species from five continents. His notable achievements include taking the big five by handgun once and the big four seven times. The collection includes fifty-nine animals that have ranked in the top ten of the SCI Record Book of Trophy Animals with sixteen ranking No. 1 with a handgun. His African collection includes nine trophy bull elephants, fifty Cape buffalo, seven leopards, and seven lions.

MOUNTED BY
HILDE TAXIDERMY
CLARKSTON, MI

SACKMAN

Alan Sackman began hunting in 1949 at the age of ten when his father, Warren, gave him his first set of guns: a single-shot 22 Springfield rifle and a single-shot 20-gauge Ithaca shotgun. Alan spent his childhood on a farm in upstate New York, which was an ideal setting for a small boy who enjoyed hunting, for there was abundant small game, such as rabbits, squirrels, woodchucks, and pheasants. Since then, he has never lost the desire to continue this fine sport.

In 1961 Alan married Barbara Lee Hefelfinger. They had three children, two sons and a daughter (all members of Safari Club International). Warren, the oldest son, recently built his own trophy room after having returned from several safaris in Africa.

In 1979, Alan and Barbara flew to Las Vegas for their first Safari Club International convention. It was there that Alan booked his first international hunt to South Africa. This was a family trip, for Allyson (their daughter) and Barbara were not yet hunters. In 1982, on a bet with Tim Otto, a professional guide in South Africa, Barbara began her hunting career by shooting zebra, impala, and sable. From that day on, her quest continues, and to date, she has hunted on all continents and taken 115 species. Alan, who enjoys hunting immensely, spends much of his time acting as assistant guide for Barbara in her pursuit for the various SCI slams. In 1997, Barbara completed her world slam of sheep, and at this time, they are the fourth couple in the world who have accomplished this task.

Mountain hunting holds a special place in the hearts of the Sackmans. Here, they find that the challenges and special beauty of these primitive areas always create exhilarating experiences and memories. Alan has taken over 150 species, and together, the Sackman's trophy room holds approximately 175 species of game from around the world.

In the fall of 1998 the Sackman hunting legacy will again be passed on when Barbara and Alan accompany the third generation of Sackmans, Carter Francis, Jr. and Warren Alan IV (already SCI Life Members) on their first safari to Africa. Hunting has brought to the Sackmans many wonderful times, along with fine and long-lasting friendships—not only with other hunters, but with outfitters and guides who have become personal friends. They thank SCI for getting them started on these monumental journeys back in 1979.

Alan & Barbara Sackman

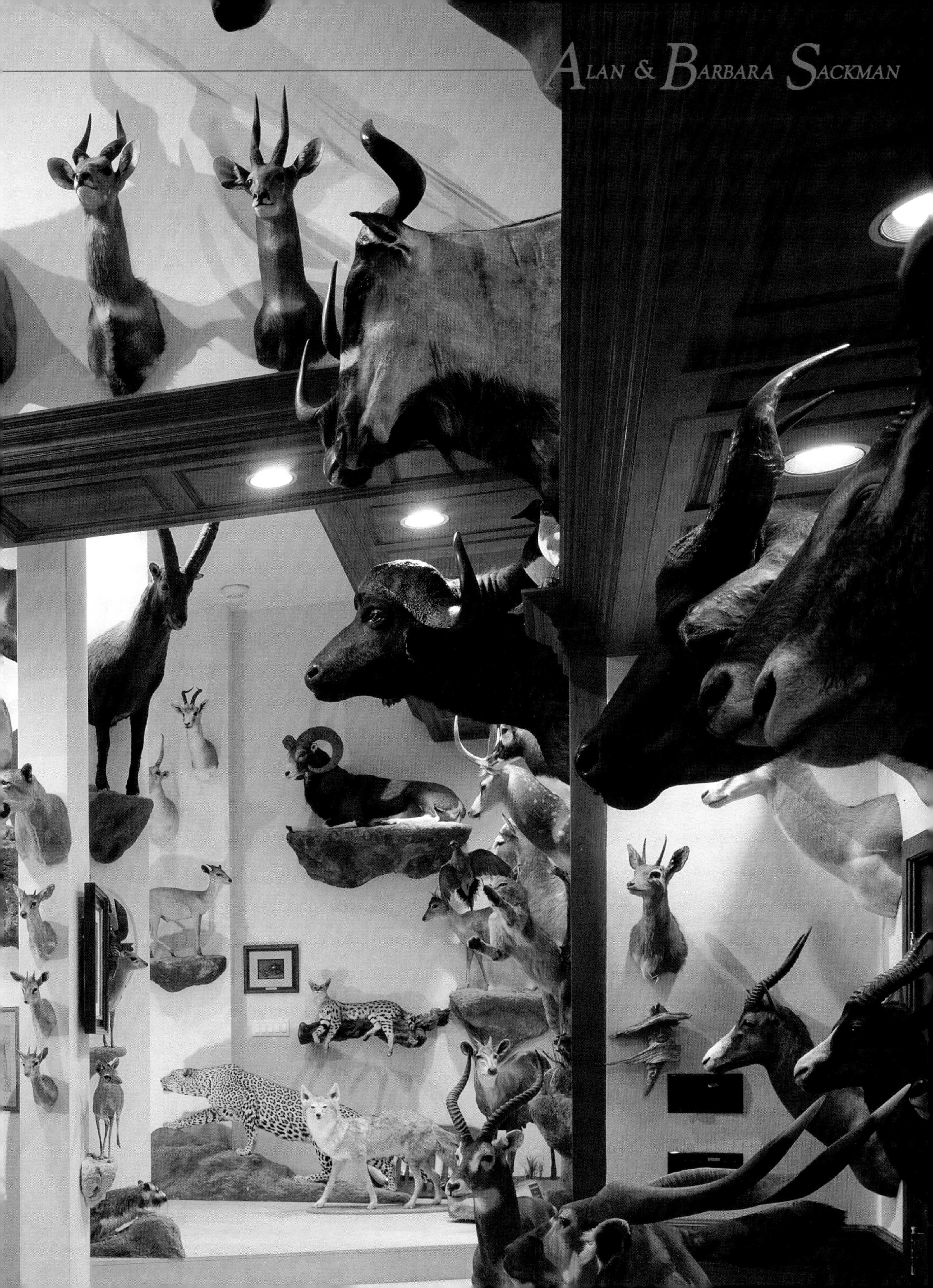

KLEIN
(1901-1974)

During the late forties, fifties, and early sixties, when worldwide big-game hunting as we know it today was in its infancy, it may well be said that no one was more the epitome of the title "trophy hunter" than Herbert Washington Klein.

As a young oil-field bookkeeper in Wyoming in the early 1930s, it somehow fell to Klein to keep the oil camps in red meat. He took to the job like a duck to water and caught the hunting fever that would, in later years, take him to the remotest corners of the earth in search of the rarest and most difficult to obtain trophies. In 1937, Klein threw away his bookkeeping eyeshade forever, secured financing, and, after some early dry holes, drilled a five-year-long string of gushers. By 1942, he was in position to pursue trophy hunting full-time and was off and running. Although he was a tireless worker and a consummate businessman, trophy hunting remained his passion until his death in August of 1974.

I first visited the Klein home and trophy room at Klein's invitation in January of 1970. His trophy room was half-circular in shape, sunken, and almost 2,000 square feet in size. The huge fireplace was in the middle of the straight wall of the room and opposite the entrance. The floors were marble and the walls were paneled in pale African teak with thirteen-foot ceilings. Klein told me on that winter evening long ago that there were 155 mounts in the room. Off the main trophy room there was an ornate bar.

What is not well known about Klein is that in addition to his known passions for sheep and African game, he was also a dedicated hunter of the world's many species of smaller wildcats. In the bar were forty-four mounts of various cats, some so exotic that I had never even heard of them. These were a mix of life-sized and shoulder mounts.

There were only two pieces of art in the room. One was a beautiful oil portrait of Klein's great friend, H.I.H. Prince Abdorezza Pahlavi of Iran. This stood on a large easel in the very center of the room. The other was a painting of a bare-breasted Mexican senorita that hung discreetly in the cat bar. It had, I believe, been given to Klein by one of his Mexican sheep hunting pals.

I believe that the photographs of the Klein trophy room within these pages were taken in the early 1960s. After my initial visit in early 1970, I had the good fortune to view it again on five subsequent occasions, the last time some six months after Klein's death. On each of these occasions, the room itself never failed to be breathtaking. To a young man very interested in big-game hunting and with the respect that I had for Mr. Klein, these times have always remained among my favorite memories.

LUCA

Renato Luca was born in 1933, and he and his wife, Maria Pia, have two sons, Alessandro and Alberto. The Lucas live in a village in the Veneto region of Italy, near Venice. Renato graduated from Padova University and afterward became an electro-technical manufacturer.

Luca has been a member of the board of directors of the SCI Italian Chapter, and he is a life member of the Safari Club International. He is also a member of the Conseil International de la Chasse de la Conservation du Gibier.

Luca has been recognized on the national and international levels for his hunting endeavors. He wrote Diari di Caccia (Hunting Diaries) The Big Five—Grand Slam, which was hailed as a remarkable success for its style and exceptional writing. This account only covers Luca's hunts over a fourteen-year period, however; so another volume will most likely be released. Like the first, the second book will reveal in even greater detail the adventure and fulfillment of hunting for game where the mountains touch the sky.

Luca's collection of sheep and goat trophies is vast. He has eight different species of argali that currently represent the most important attraction of his collection. His many safaris around the world have allowed him to collect some of the most exquisite birds and animals, which Luca has placed in the trophy rooms of his Veneta Villa. Visitors not only have the opportunity to admire his 1,400 trophies, but they also can view the charming ambiance and architecture of his Italian-style trophy rooms.

In these rooms one will find a bird collection totaling over 1,000 different species found in Europe. Other animals are divided by continents, and they are placed in two different parts of the villa: the private museum where only full-size animals appear and the trophy room where only horns and heads are placed. Renato Luca is also a collector of shotguns, antique books, prints from Audubon, Gould, Selby, and Manetti, and bronze statues of wild animals—all as distinctive as the personality of their owner. Luca welcomes all hunters and admirers to come and enjoy his collection.

UNDERDAHL

I believe that each hunter's trophy room is an extension of his lifestyle. So, rather than build a trophy room at my home, where I spend very little time, I decided that my office would be a perfect setting for my trophies.

In 1972, I acquired the French mansion in Minneapolis built by the Pillsbury Flour Milling family for their daughter as a wedding present. After several years' work and many unexpected expenses, it has been restored to its original architectural splendor. The fine craftsmanship of 1910-1915 makes my office an attractive "base camp." There are forty-two rooms, most of which display my trophies. The photos you see are of the larger ones. I have taken over 300 big-game trophies, with over 125 species in the SCI record book.

I grew up in rural northern Minnesota where my father's credo was work hard and then go hunting and fishing—but spend more time hunting and fishing than working! In 1943 I joined the U.S. Navy and made seventeen opposed landings throughout the Pacific. After the war, I came back to Minnesota to work, hunt, and fish. I made hunts in all the big-game areas of North America. I joined the California chapter of the SCI soon after. My membership number was 68, and by coincidence, my grand slam number is 68 in the North American Sheep Hunters Association.

In 1969 I made my first safari to Africa. Since then, I've made seventeen safaris to Africa, hunted in Russia, Spain, England, South America, New Zealand, Australia, Mexico, all Canadian Provinces, and all the "big game" states in the U.S.

On my first brown bear hunt in 1967, I took one in the top ten SCI, and earlier in 1965 my polar bear was also in the top ten. I've taken over ninety deer and fifty antelope. Some of my trophies are great, some small, and some in-between, but each is a trophy that evokes respect for the animal and memories that can never be duplicated.

In 1986, I donated forty-seven trophies to the James Ford Bell Museum of Natural History at the University of Minnesota. This donation established a touch and feel program that continues today.

In 1954 I started Pinecrest, a custom architectural door, mantel, and shutter manufacturing company that specializes in quality installations internationally. For over twenty years, I've donated my products through our national SCI conventions and many local chapters for fundraising. This has generated in excess of $100,000 over the years for conservation.

For me, life must be a challenge with unknown expectations, and this is why I hunt. I could try to describe the inspirations that mountains, valleys, lakes, and forests have created in my mind, but I think I will leave that to the great writers. I would like to end this with a bit of my personal philosophy: Your three greatest hunts are your first, your last, and your next.

JAKSICK

A lifetime resident of the state of Nevada, Sam Jaksick developed the passion for the hunt early in life. He hunted deer and waterfowl in the late '50s, but the possibility of a big-game hunt in Canada, Alaska, or Africa was beyond his pocketbook . . . and his years. He often heard his family and older friends remark that someday they were going to travel or someday they were going to hunt exotic places, but due to their age, physical condition, or lack of money, that "someday" never came. This made quite an impression on Sam, and upon graduating from the University of Nevada he decided that one way or another his "someday" was going to start right then.

In 1963 he got together enough money to go on his first big-game hunt outside of Nevada—a polar bear hunt in Alaska with outfitter Ron Hayes. After that hunt Sam never looked back. His next hunt was a safari to Mozambique in 1965.

As Sam's real estate development and gaming business began to prosper, the number of his hunts increased. In the late '60s and early '70s Sam traveled to numerous areas around the world—many not previously hunted, including the mid-Altai in Mongolia and remote parts of the African continent.

Sam has hunted in Africa on fourteen separate safaris as well as numerous hunts in Asia, Europe, and North and South America. He has over one hundred mounted trophies and has another fifty in storage or in various stages of being mounted. His animals are not all located in one trophy room, but rather are displayed in his home at Lake Tahoe, his office, and his cattle ranch in northern Nevada.

Sam has always been very selective in the trophies he has taken. He believes the real challenge of a hunt is to stalk close enough to the animal to evaluate the horn or antler size carefully and if the animal is not exceptionally large for that species, leave it for another time. He particularly enjoys field scoring sheep, pronghorn antelope, and mule deer.

Over his hunting career, Sam has taken thirty sheep from around the world, has three Grand Slams, and a Super Slam. His North American Grand Slam has the third highest total combined score for the four species of Boone & Crockett sheep. Sam has received numerous awards for trophies listed in Boone & Crockett as well as African, Asian, and North American animals listed in SCI's record book.

Sam has always enjoyed hunting with his children, Stan, Wendy, and Todd. Several years ago Sam accompanied his fourteen-year old son Todd on four North American sheep hunts, and watched him complete his Grand Slam. On a recent safari to Tanzania, he went along only as an observer while Todd did the hunting. Sam feels it's important for children to develop an appreciation for hunting and the great outdoors. He says: "There's something about sitting around a campfire at night with your son discussing the day's hunt that's hard to duplicate."

V AN D OREN

My beloved husband is where he longs to be most of the time—on the hunt. He has commissioned me, his Zimbabwean wife, who writes English better than he, to write this essay about his passion, one that I share and understand.

Bernard started hunting thirty years ago. Like most amateur hunters, he hunted the local French countryside for wild boar, fox, and red deer. The fever soon took hold of his heart and soul, and he became anxious to hunt elsewhere and to look upon different horizons where different species scatter the landscape. He went on his first African safari in 1981 in the CAR. Since then, my husband hunts at least once a year in Africa, and has harvested most of the big species there. He has acquired more than seventy buffalo, which is by far his favourite game, the biggest (fifty inches) having been shot in Zimbabwe in 1989, the year that we met. He has hunted approximately fifteen lions and about as many leopards. Elephant hunting is also one of his all-time favourites, and he has hunted ten elephants in various countries, including Ethiopia, where he also obtained a superb mountain nyala, as well as an SCI World Record beisa oryx. His tusk collection is rather impressive: One pair weighs in at 80 pounds on one side and 79 on the other—quite an achievement in today's world.

Besides his yearly African safaris, he also hunts red stag in Poland every September without fail—this is a ritual dating from 1975. He has collected over this period of time eighty-two exceptional stag.

Other hunting destinations have included Tajikistan, where he obtained a 56-inch Marco Polo, Mongolia, Russia, Austria, Uzbekistan, and Brazil. He has hunted argali three times in the Altai, being successful on all occasions, with all three measuring over 60 inches. He has also hunted the elusive markhor. He says that his passion for hunting has enabled him to travel the world, and most of all, enabled him to visit places that are not your common tourist destinations—wild and unexploited places. In Alaska he hunted a ten-foot brown bear, and in the Arctic he managed to shoot an eleven-foot polar bear under terrible weather conditions.

My husband is a hunter of the old school, believing in fair chase hunting. He tracks and walks after his prey, alone, whenever possible. His skill and experience as a hunter have put luck on his side, and most of the animals he has hunted are of exceptional trophy quality. My husband continues to hunt—his future destinations are as far and wide and exotic as those of the past. And I, his wife, will either accompany him on certain hunts as I have in the past, or I shall be at home with the architects, planning the expansion of our house to make room for the new trophies!

YURÉN

I was born on 25 November 1942, in Mexico City, Mexico, and raised by my loving parents, Senator Jesús and Blanca Yurén. By the time I was sixteen, I had shot my first big-game animal, a white-tailed deer. My beloved wife, Pita, and I were married in 1966. She has been my partner since then in the continuous adventure that has been our life, including many hunting trips. We have raised three children of whom we are very proud and have three wonderful grandchildren.

Hunting has been a way of life for us. We have traveled the world in its pursuit. In our search we have collected 296 species of big game that are represented in nearly five hundred mounts within our collection.

Over the years I have received many hunting awards. Some of them include: the Luchador Olmeca, to the best sportsman; the Salón de la Fama (Hall of Fame) from the Mexican Sports Confederation; the North American Grand Slam of Wild Sheep; the ISHA Super Slam of the World Wild Sheep; the SCI International Hunter of the Year; and the Weatherby Award—the greatest award in the hunting world. I am indeed fortunate to be honored with these awards for doing what I like best.

For the true sportsman, hunting is a great love between hunter and prey. It is a love so unique that the prey gives its own life to be introduced into immortality. Prey and hunter merge in the moment of the collection and remain there forever. It is a philosophic, mystic, and esoteric relationship. It is a mystery that can only be solved by those initiated in the liturgy of hunting.

The trophy room is the tangible embodiment of this relationship. It is a tribute to the beauty and handsomeness of the game, kept by men in imitation of the beauty already provided by the Lord in nature. In this sense, trophies serve as everlasting remainders of the mystical relationship between hunter and hunted. Each trophy also reveals its beauty to those who don't have the privilege to admire it in its own habitat, teaching us that one must hunt in order to conserve.

I dislike measuring game, although I have had to do it often. The trophies themselves have such greatness that in truth they cannot be compared. For every hunter, his or her trophies will be the best because they represent personal memories of prey taken in fair chase. Deeply carved in one of the wooden beams of my trophy room are the words that the Spanish poet José Zorrilla has spoken through one of his characters, Don Juan. With these same words I dedicate my trophy room to my trophies: "No os podéis quejar de mi, vosotros a quien maté, si buena vida os quité, mejor sepultura os di." ("Those killed by me must not complain, if a good life I took away, it is a better grave I give you today.")

POWELL-COTTON
(1866-1940)

Major Percy Horace Gordon Powell-Cotton was born in 1866 in England, the eldest son of H. H. Powell-Cotton. Powell-Cotton was the personification of the British Victorian gentleman of leisure so prevalent during the height of the British Empire. From 1887 until 1939 he traveled on twenty-eight expeditions to Asia and Africa in search of specimens for his collection. From his many journeys abroad, Powell-Cotton amassed one of the finest personal collections of specimens in England during the latter part of the nineteenth and early part of the twentieth centuries. He housed his specimens in the family estate, Quex Park, in Kent, which he inherited in 1894 and which eventually became filled with trophy animals. After WW II, Quex Park was turned into a museum that is open to the public and funded by a trust established by Powell-Cotton.

A number of animal species and subspecies were named after Powell-Cotton, including a giraffe and the northern white rhino (Ceratotherium simum cottoni). His accomplishments are many, but he will always be remembered as the man who collected the second largest tusks ever recorded (198 and 174 pounds) in 1906, near Lake Albert in the Congo.

Among his other achievements, he was the author of two books on hunting, In Unknown Africa and A Sporting Trip Through Abyssinia, both of which are much sought after by hunters and book collectors. From both a publishing and taxidermy standpoint, Powell-Cotton's relationship with Rowland Ward was pivotal. It was Ward who shaped Powell-Cotton's trophy collection, and it was Ward who published Powell-Cotton's first book.

Powell-Cotton was accompanied on many of his expeditions by his wife, who died in 1964. They were married in Nairobi in 1905, and their honeymoon was a trip to Uganda and the Congo. On most of his African trips, he used a Mannlicher bolt-action rifle for plains game and a .400 double barrel by Jeffery for large game. On a trip to Central Africa in 1906, he was attacked by a lion, and it was entirely due to the bravery of some of his trackers that he escaped with only minor wounds. Like most Victorian gentlemen of leisure, he was a member of the Royal Geographical Society and the London Zoological Society. He died in 1940.

SCHERRER

I was born 2 September 1931 in Rorschach, Switzerland. When I was about thirteen years old, I shot my first big-game animal, a roe deer. I then started hunting red stag and chamois. It was not until much later that I would hunt alpine ibex. When I was twenty-two, I left Switzerland—my father had died and I thought America would be a great place to start a new life.

My parents owned a meat-packing plant in Switzerland, and I had been trained as a butcher and sausage maker. I was immediately offered a job at the Hoffman Packing Company in Los Angeles; this was 1954. Three years later I started my own meat-distributing company; within five years I owned five trucks. In 1968 I decided I wanted to get into a new business so that I could take time off now and then for hunting. My next venture was in the car-wash business, and it also became very successful.

My first hunting trips out of California were to Idaho, Wyoming, and Canada. Then I went to Angola in 1970. I have been on about twenty-five safaris and have collected all the spiral-horned antelope of Africa, including the giant eland I shot in the CAR, and the bongo I took in the southern Sudan with José Simoes. I have also taken the Big Five—I got my elephant in the Sudan, with ivory of 102 pounds and 97 pounds.

In the Middle East I have hunted Iran twice—the first time in 1975 with the amazing guide Massih Kia—and was one of the last to hunt Marco Polo sheep in Afghanistan. In Mongolia I got the Gobi argali and the Altai argali. Other memorable hunts include Nepal, Siberia for snow sheep, Belograd for red stag and sagia antelope, Russia proper for wild boar, and the Caucasus Mountains for tur. I have acquired the Super Grand Slam and American Grand Slam of sheep, as well as the North America 27. Sheep is my favorite game animal.

In South America I have hunted in Venezuela for jaguar and Argentina for taruca. In Europe I have hunted in Hungary, Spain, Austria, Poland for European bison and red stag, and England for the Pere Davis deer. My collection of animals from Australia and New Zealand includes about 250 to 260 species. If I had one last chance to hunt, I would like to hunt the Ovis ammon karelini in Russia or China.

My 18,600-square-foot home in Brentwood contained a 6,000-square-foot trophy room to accommodate my 200 mounted heads and 150 life-size animals. I am married to Grace, and we have two adult children: John (23) and Elizabeth (31).

I donated my animals to the Museum of Natural History in Las Vegas so that many people, especially children, would have the opportunity to see my collection of species from six continents. All of my animals are there now, except for my Marco Polo sheep trophy that I kept for my son. Since his birth sign is a ram, this particular trophy was special to him.

SEDANO

After more than fourteen safaris across Sudan, Zambia, and Cameroon, my African collection is practically complete except for two great voids: the mountain nyala and the yellow-backed duiker. The first one is absent because I missed the target (I hope to get it on my next safari), and the second is gone because I couldn't see it (except for its footprints)!

The collection is the result of twenty-four safaris (336 suffering days) over seventeen years, 1980 to 1996. I went on my first African safari when I was thirty-two, in the Sudan on a twenty-eight day safari. I had bad luck on this first occasion and bagged no bongo, yellow-backed duiker, elephant, or buffalo. I repeated the safari three months later, but again had no luck, except with the elephant. It was not until my third safari in RSA in 1982 that my collection was truly born. There, I met Fred Rademeyer (who was my same age) and, even though my English was very poor, our synergetic comprehension was instantaneous.

After twenty-three days on safari, the results were thrilling. I bagged two No. 1 trophies, a rhino and leopard (according to the SCI and Rowland Ward books), and I also acquired a series of other marvelous trophies. It was Fred who helped me join SCI and enter my trophies. He also taught me not to fire at every animal I see, and to kill only the really exceptional trophies—and this has been my hunting philosophy ever since.

In short, in my trophy room you can admire 112 species (most of them mounted by Nico Van Rooyen) with some exceptional leopard trophies, a 33 ½" bongo, a 32" sitatunga, a Cape buffalo with a 22" boss, waterbuck, reedbuck, wildebeest, eland, wild pig, dik-dik, sassaby, pygmy antelope, and many more!

ARLISI

After my father died when I was six years old, my brother and I moved from upstate New York to Los Angeles, with our strong, caring mother. Not long after moving to LA, I saw my first taxidermist shop. In the window was a hunting knife with a handle made of a deer hoof. It was the most beautiful thing I had ever seen, totally desirable—and totally unobtainable. That memory is indelibly imprinted on my mind, as clear now as it was the day it happened.

I know of no other hunters in my family, but soon after I turned twelve, my brother and I got the fever and started setting traps in the open and lush Hollywood hills. We killed and skinned a rattlesnake, salted the skin, and nailed it to a redwood board, and this was my first trophy. Our mother gave us a closet in which we hung the cured snake and not long after, that closet was covered with rabbit skins, squirrel skins, hawk feathers, and anything else we could shoot with a BB gun. This was my first trophy room, though I certainly did not know it at the time.

In 1945, at age twenty, I was discharged from the service, and I bought my first car. It was then that my hunting expanded to the California deserts. All my free time and money went into hunting, rifles, and shotguns in order to shoot bigger game. Even then the challenge, the excitement, and the sharing that is an integral part of every hunt filled my life. My wife sees my hunting as an underlying necessity to my well-being, and she must be right, for a prerequisite for any home we have ever owned has always been that it must have walls high enough to accommodate my trophies. After a little work and a great deal of luck, I finally built a real trophy room in 1981 for my North American game. When my hunting became global, I built a second one, primarily for African animals. (The room is shown in this publication).

Hunting has been a part of me for as long as I can remember—an innate drive that was as natural as breathing. Every hunter knows there are no words that can adequately describe what drives us to return to the outdoors time and again. The friendships forged and the excitement encountered are only a part of it. The passion can only be understood by those who share it, and by those who love the animals they hunt.

Most hunters wonder what will become of their trophies when they are gone, but without my even having mentioned it, my hunting son, Don, and his son, have told me that my trophies will be kept and appreciated for the duration of their lifetimes. I think that the majority of us who have the trophy hunter mentality would consider this the ultimate gift. I certainly do.

WILLIAMS

Having been raised in rural Virginia, I was, from an early age, an avid hunter. After finishing college, I joined the U.S. Marine Corps, and after extensive training, served thirteen months in Vietnam. Upon my return home, however, I decided I was no longer fond of guns, nor of the hunt. This attitude stayed with me until 1986, when I was diagnosed with a benign brain tumor, and underwent a serious operation. While recovering, my wife Kris brought me a book, Safari, The Last Adventure by Peter Hathaway Capstick. Sixty days after my release from the hospital, Kris and I were on safari in Zimbabwe. To date, we have completed twenty-four African safaris, and have hunted extensively on six continents.

I became so hooked on African hunting that I went on twenty-three safaris in just nine years, collecting most of the African trophy species. My hunting interests expanded to include the remotest destinations in the world, and my trophy room filled quickly, necessitating building a second room that I use for my non-African trophies. Although each trophy room can accommodate more than 100 trophies, I limit the new room to about 60 or 70, and rotate the species displayed with ones I have stored.

My hunting itineraries have been guided by the SCI World Hunting Awards programs. In 1998, I became only the eighteenth person to have achieved the SCI Crowing Achievement, which recognizes the number and quality of worldwide trophy species collected. Additionally, hard work and good luck have enabled me to obtain 21 inner circles (6 diamond level); 10 of 12 SCI slams; and the Fourth Pinnacle of Achievement.

I am frequently asked by visitors which hunt was the best—"All of them" is my answer. When I quietly sit in my trophy room, I relive each and every hunt. Several times each year, I invite church and school groups to visit, and use those opportunities to help young girls and boys understand the relationship of hunting to conservation. Teaching young people the paradox that most hunters have both a great love and respect for wildlife and the wilderness is a bit complicated, but a very rewarding use of the trophy rooms. I do not try to make anyone a hunter, but I do try to prevent them from becoming an antihunter.

I am currently planning to host my first "Sensory Safari" by inviting a group of sight-impaired adults and children to visit my trophy rooms. My lectures and stories will concentrate on my sixty-plus life-size mounts. I very much look forward to sharing through words, as they touch and feel the trophies, some of the exciting adventures I have had. As the great man once said about a cigar, a trophy room is not just a trophy room!

BIGG

My wife, Meredith, and I live in the 1775 home in which I was raised (without electricity until I was thirteen), and that belonged to my farming parents before me. Out of one window, there is a view of my elementary school (one room, eight grades), and out another, the building where Meredith and I both attended high school. I worked my way through Dartmouth College and through law school, deriving my primary income from a job as a Registered Maine Guide. Consequently, in the early years I had neither the money nor the space to properly full-life mount many trophies—my jaguar, Arctic wolf, and many record-book spearfishing trophies.

Meredith was born in Turner, Maine. We met, fell in love, and married comparatively late in life (I was 49 and she was 34), but we still have had plenty of time to rack up a world of experiences, and Meredith has accompanied me on most of my hunting trips. The buildings that once housed hay, cows, horses, grain, milking equipment, hens, pigs, and turkeys—and at one time, an antique store and hundreds of collectibles—are bursting with a lifetime's collection of specimens from Canada, the High Arctic, Mexico, the western U.S., Spain, South Africa, Botswana, Zambia, Zimbabwe, Namibia, and elsewhere. Life-size elephants, rhinos, crocodiles, Cape buffaloes, leopards, lions, and hippos (only shoulder mount) mingle with grizzly and other bears, moose, mountain sheep, and goats.

We have redesigned very little of the property, but with Meredith's unerring decorator's eye at work, every one of the unheated and uncooled rooms that house our trophies has been turned into a comfortable and attractive sitting room where we can sip a drink together, or with friends, and reminisce. The ancient, weathered boards that make up the old barn and attached sheds are also home to artifacts from half a lifetime of underwater archaeology, wreck diving, and spear and line fishing.

Although I have never hunted for the record book, I have been exceedingly fortunate to garner forty-two trophy class entries, and several of the first, second, third, and fourth places are among the collection in the barn. I also have predominantly hunted with a black-powder muzzle (all of my African hunts have been with this weapon), and several years ago I was honored by being inducted into the SCI Muzzleloaders Hall of Fame. The hunt is still far from over for Meredith and me. We are anxiously awaiting the arrival of our Canadian bear, and later this year we will pursue a bongo in Cameroon.

We open our doors to over two thousand people a year, many are school children and scouts, and we love to share our memories and magnificent beasts with the public. The next time you're in town, come see us!

BRANDT

Captain John Brandt's credo is that a dedicated hunter must be an ardent conservationist, for no one has a more vested interest in the preservation of game animals than the hunter.

Over a half century ago, John Brandt took his first step toward becoming a big-game hunter when, to everyone's surprise, he hit a running rabbit at thirty-five paces with his BB gun! During his university years, under the GI Bill, he progressed to mule deer, elk, and pronghorn, and became a subsistence hunter in order to feed his family.

The next thirty years he spent on a number of varied assignments in the military and for the U.S. government, including serving as a special agent in the Counter Intelligence Corps; counter insurgency consultant for the U.S. State Department, and environmental biologist for the USPHS Indian Service. Much of his adult life was spent in Southeast Asia on the Malay Peninsula and Indochina, back when the lush rain forests were still in abundance and filled with wildlife. During those years, before overpopulation and greed destroyed much of the natural environment, Brandt had numerous run-ins with man-eating tigers, man-mauling leopards, and rogue elephants, all detailed in his books, Hunters of Man, Asian Hunter, and Horned Giants.

Returning to the United States after the Vietnam War ended, Brandt joined the fledgling Safari Club International and became a chapter president, regional vice president, and national vice president. He also held responsibilities as chairman of the Trophy Records Committee and helped to develop the internationally accepted SCI scoring system and the SCI record book. He has received the SCI President's Award, the SCI Chairman's Award, and the SCI Award for Outstanding Editorial Contribution.

After extensive hunting in tropical Asia for his favorite game animal, the giant gaur (or seladang), as well as tiger, banteng, and water buffalo in the 1950s and 1960s, he made his first African safari for three weeks to the old Tanganyika Territory at a cost of only $2,400! He has subsequently made sixteen safaris to Africa, and has hunted on all the continents: from Siberia to Malaya, from the Arctic to Argentina, from Australia to Mongolia, and from Europe to India—with many other locations along the way that are now either closed to hunting or rarely hunted. He completed his American Sheep Grand Slam in 1996.

During his long hunting career, Brandt has successfully collected over 140 species of big game animals with over 80 in the record books, including three No. 1s, and four in the top ten.

In recent years, as a museum research zoologist, Brandt has been involved with the ongoing identification of the amazing, newly discovered large animals from Vietnam and Laos. His collections are in several national museums, and his trophy collection is destined for a public museum to promote interest in wildlife.

In 1982 he retired from U.S. government service and has recorded his many hunting adventures in his latest, and last, book entitled Soul of the Hunter—A Half Century of Big-Game Hunting.

SHAH

When I built my house three years ago, I specifically designed it to accommodate my 300-plus trophies. These mementos are displayed in a variety of mounts that I arranged in my living room. In addition I have established my own wildlife museum in Sumatra that houses approximately 200 species of wildlife. I have three employees who maintain the condition of my trophies. There is no charge to enter the museum, which has attracted many educational groups and visitors from abroad.

My hunting activities started when I was a boy following in my father's footsteps, and I've always hoped that my children would do the same. With this in mind, as well as my love for wildlife, I have been promoting conservation and have supported projects and seminars that teach the concept of conservation through game hunting, and how it benefits future generations.

I am the chairman of YASRI (an environmental group) whose aim is to preserve our wildlife and its habitat. My homeland of Indonesia is a very big country composed of 13,000 islands. The country has a wide variety of wildlife including the one-horned rhino and the Komodo dragon.

I was appointed by the Hunting and Shooting Association (a government-run association) to pioneer sport hunting by using the SCI concept of "conservation by utilization," a topic about which I often lecture. The Indonesian government had planned to open safari hunting immediately, but due to the recent political and economic crises it had to be delayed. In the meantime, my friends and I are planning to open an SCI chapter this year, and I am helping develop the rules and regulations.

My hunting activities for the past ten years have been varied: I have hunted in Australia, New Zealand, South Africa, Tanzania, Zambia, the U.S., Canada, and the Yukon. In 1995 I was the first Indonesian to achieve the Big Five Award and was very fortunate to shoot all five in the same year (1995). The rhino was taken in South Africa and the rest in Tanzania. Other awards I have received since 1990 are: SCI Inner Circle and Grand Slam Awards (1994); SCI World Hunting Award (1994); and the Bronze, Copper, Silver, and Gold Awards for sheep. I am a master measurer and a life member of SCI and IPHA (International Professional Hunting Association). Every year I attend the SCI convention in the U.S., which gives me a chance to meet other hunters and share experiences.

I started my business (rubber, palm oil, real estate, and aluminum manufacturing) at a very young age, and now 75 percent of my time is spent on social and charitable activities. Recently, I refurbished the state-owned zoo and have added many animals. My aim is again educational: I want to educate the public to respect animals and their habitat as a means of saving threatened species from extinction. I am subsidizing the zoo, and I am happy to do it. We accept both live animals for our zoo and trophies for the wildlife museum attached to it.

BABOON
AFRICA

'RAHMAT TROPHIES'
MEDAN-INDONESIA

MAHARAJAHS

As a class of people, probably nobody in the world brought forth more enthusiastic hunters than India's ruling princes; indeed, some might even say that this group was obsessed with hunting. Up to 1947, under British administration, Indian rulers could collect taxes in their own fiefdoms, and this enabled the maharajahs, rajas, nizams, and other Indian rulers to indulge in whims and luxuries that by today's standards could only be called stupendous. It was probably stated without much exaggeration that from the turn of the century till the start of WW II the Indian nobility who visited London kept the order ledgers of London's gun trade filled all by themselves. These men of unparalleled wealth ordered the finest double rifles imaginable, sometimes in pairs and even in sets of three. The engraving and other embellishments were done in gold and, sometimes, diamonds, and were so ornate they have never been equaled. In addition, the Indian ruling elite spurred the English gun trade to develop ever more different nitro express calibers so that they could bring something unusual home to talk about with the maharajah in the next palace. After WW II, however, their world went into decline. When the Indian government reneged on its promise of financial support in the 1960s, the wealth of the ruling princes of India declined rapidly.

While there were literally dozens and dozens of palaces that had trophies at one time, there are now only very few places left that have anything resembling a trophy collection. Two factors have played a major role in the decline of great trophy collections in India: First of all is the physical climate, which is extremely hot in the summer and is unbearably humid during the rainy season—neither conductive to the longevity of mounted tigers or gaur. In conjunction with the physical climate is the problem created by the relentless attack of insects; rarely do trophies survive these insidious pests. The second factor is the political climate. Since the hunting ban of the early 1970s, hunting has gone out of fashion. Recently a minister of the national government publicly burned old hunting trophies to make a statement. In this political climate many people have disposed of the trophies of their ancestors.

We have depicted in this section of the book some of the rooms that can still be found in modern-day India. The great numbers of tiger are largely gone, the herds of wild elephant have severely declined, and the population of the great Indian wild ox, the gaur, has been confined to a few areas—this in a land where these animals were at one time plentiful, largely because of hunting. When the Indian government did its much vaunted "inventory" of its wildlife in the late 1960s, it found the greatest amount of game in the hunting reserves of the maharajahs—a fact that should be interesting to both hunters and nonhunters alike. Many of these areas were subsequently taken over by the government and made into parks and sanctuaries in order to protect what was left of India's once-great populations of wildlife. Few people realize today as they enter India's parks and reserves that had it not been for the proclivity of the maharajahs for hunting India's wildlife would be all but gone.

LACK

I am an African—my family has lived in Africa for over two hundred years. Apart from a brief flirtation with North America and Europe, I have confined my hunting to Africa and, in particular, to southern Africa.

Having said that, I have hunted assiduously since the age of nine on literally hundreds of occasions in eight African countries and am passionate (my wife says obsessive) about this amazing pastime. I say pastime, not hobby, on purpose, as hunting is a pervasive influence in my life: I collect books on hunting; almost all the artwork I own depicts wildlife scenes; I write articles on hunting for magazines and a collection of these articles is soon to be published in book form; I teach youngsters to hunt; I am a member of eight hunting and conservation associations; I am a trustee of the World Wildlife Fund of southern Africa; I am a game rancher and chairman of Karoo Safaris, which, as the name implies, is an African safari outfitter. In short, my entire life is inextricably interwoven with hunting.

My life of hunting has followed a well-trodden path from the little boy who was only too happy to hunt anything that moved to culling and meat hunting, and from hunting general game to trophy big-game hunting for those special and difficult specimens that Africa has to offer, like the big five, bongo, mountain nyala, and Lord Derby eland. I now enjoy hunting for the sake of hunting and teaching youngsters to hunt.

I have never entered an animal of mine in a record book and have ambivalent feelings in this regard. On the one hand, I like to have the record books as references and enjoy shooting good trophies that score well, but, on the other hand, I am concerned that the competitive element inherently created by such books can lead to unethical conduct harmful to hunting, and demeaning and degrading to hunter and wildlife alike.

I hope my trophies will be seen within this framework. They are my memories, my mementos. I collect them and keep them, but not necessarily because they are all big. Some are and some are not. But they all serve as reminders of my hunts—of successes and failures, of good times and bad. Because I have hunted every game animal in South Africa and all but a handful in southern Africa, not to keep them would be a shame and a waste. I have outgrown the study that you see pictured here, and am busy moving these trophies, plus an additional forty that are currently housed by my taxidermist, to a new trophy room on my game ranch, Bankfontein, in the Agtersneeuberg Nature Reserve in the Karoo.

This reserve, which my friends and I have helped create, is the largest private nature reserve proclaimed by Act of Parliament in South Africa and is home to twenty-three different species of antelope. I am much prouder to be associated with this venture than I am of any or all of my trophies and my hunting exploits.

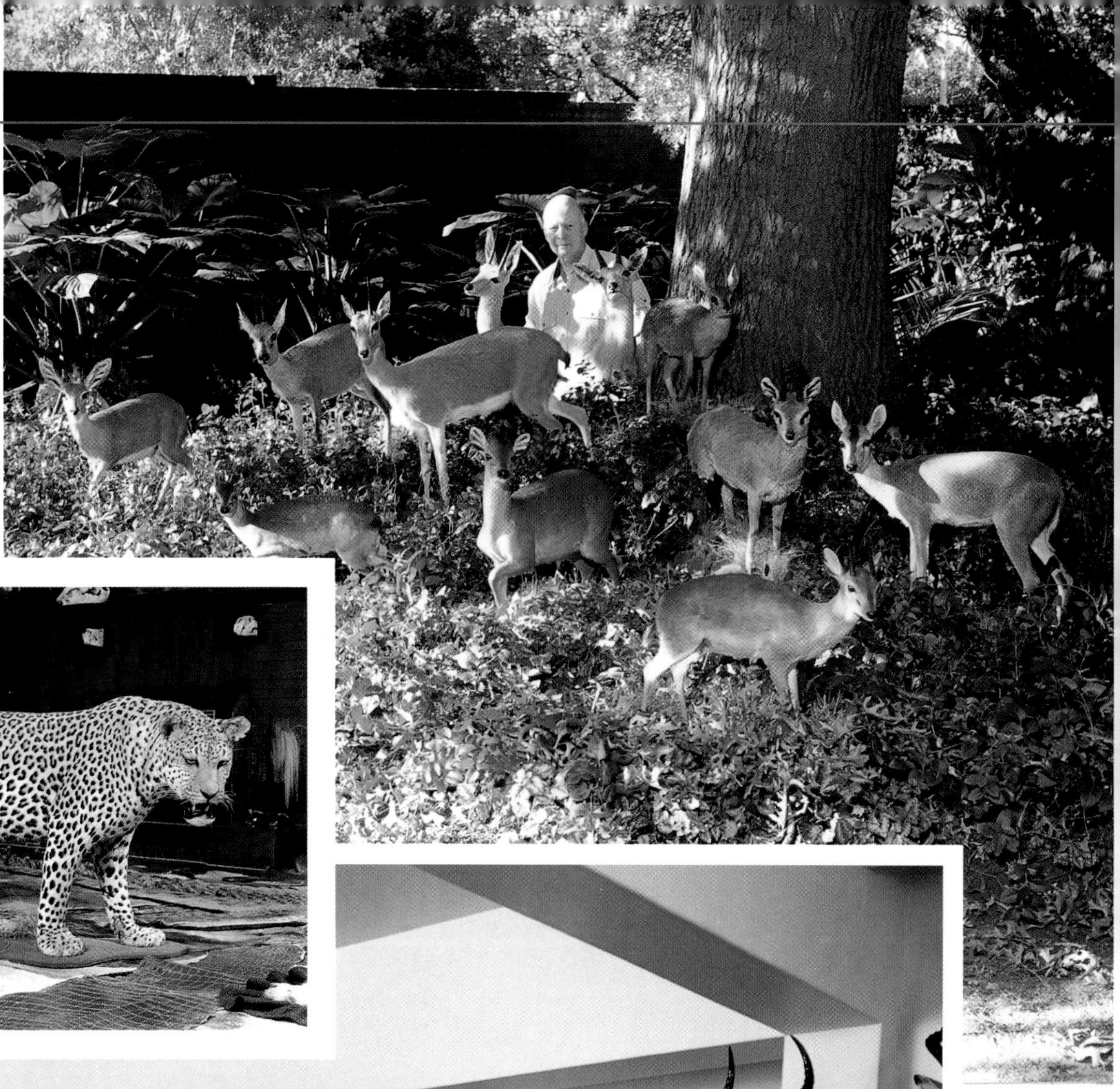

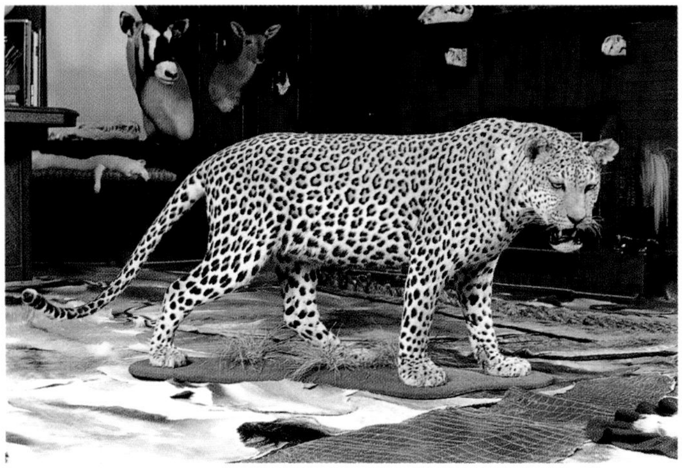

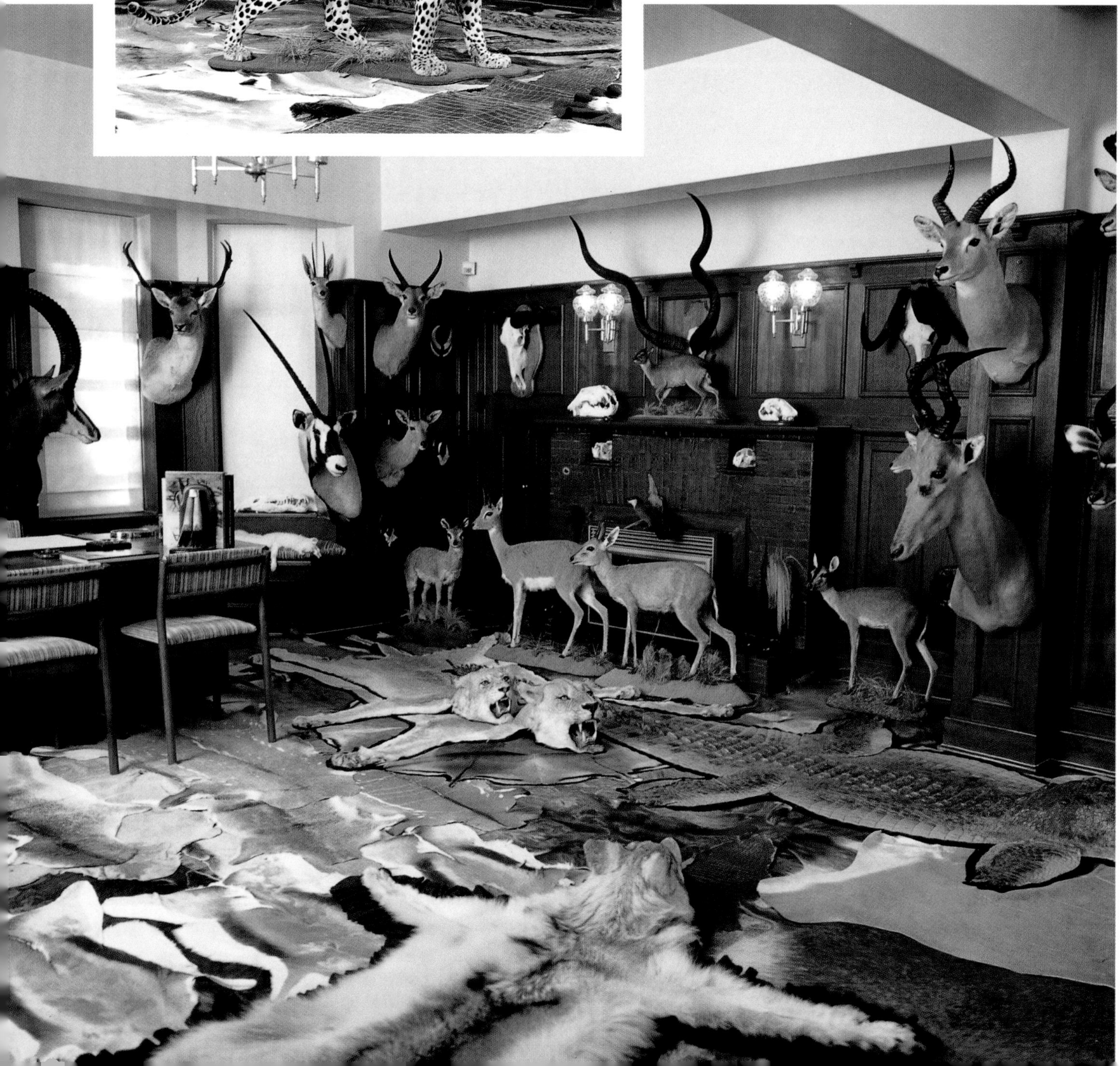

LOGAN

Growing up in southern Saskatchewan, I did a little birdhunting with my dad, and after moving to Alberta in 1968, I went on my first elk hunt in the Panther River area. In 1978, a Dall sheep in the Northwest Territory was my first taste of sheep hunting, and the start of twenty years of various experiences around the world.

I have collected twenty-six sheep (twenty-two species), a Grand Slam in 1986, and a Super Slam in 1991. I hope to add two additional species in 1998 (Kamchatka and Tajikistan). Along the way I have collected most of the North American species and have my first African hunt planned for 1999 in Zimbabwe.

I designed my trophy room with an entire wall dedicated to my collection of wild sheep of the world. Other space is filled with trophies my wife, Marion, and I have taken.

I used a cherry wood wainscoting with a one-foot ledge to display smaller trophies, photos, and collectibles. I have a matching bookcase and gun cabinet that contrast nicely with the green marble countertop and fireplace. The walls are twelve feet high and the ceiling reaches to fifteen feet. At the peak hangs a handmade elk-antler chandelier-fan (all drops from the famous Panther River Valley) that provides excellent light and air circulation.

The room was to be a functional, not strictly personal, museum. I spend many evenings here playing bridge with the boys or just drinking wine by the fireplace and reminiscing.

Local craftsmen have contributed much to the ambiance of the room. The woodwork was done by Tony Poropat; most of the taxidermy is by Tony Cassar of Alpine Taxidermy; most of the bronzes are by Rick Taylor; and the photography is by Colin Michie of Photovisions. They have done a truly beautiful job!

Our home was built west of Calgary, Alberta, in order to take advantage of the magnificent view and to allow me easy access to my office where I work in the oil patch. I am within driving distance of some of my favorite hunting spots, and I have an international airport nearby for connections to some of the far-off game fields I have enjoyed around the world.

G. SEQUEIRA

Born in Madrid in 1940, Marcial G. Sequeira has been married for thirty-one years to Maite; the Sequeiras have two daughters, Monica and Marta, and one grandson—who Marcial hopes will one day become his ardent hunting companion. Although not born into a hunting family, G. Sequeira began his hunting career at an early age in his homeland of Spain.

His studies in medicine and his career as a doctor and entrepreneur at home precluded G. Sequeira from hunting abroad until 1971, when he first traveled to Mozambique. Since then he has been obsessed by the "call of Africa" and has returned to that continent forty-five times, hunting in thirteen countries, some of which have subsequently closed their doors to hunting.

G. Sequeira has collected fourteen big elephant trophies, six of them weighing over a hundred pounds. The last one he obtained on his second safari with his daughter Marta when she was ten. Since that time, he has ceased hunting the wonderful pachyderm, concluding that his elephant tally was sufficient and there was no need to risk the extinction of such a magnificent animal.

A few years later in 1982, his obsession with mountain hunting (wild sheep and goats) kicked in, and he was awarded his first Super Slam. Since then he has collected 29 wild sheep, 24 wild goats, and 10 wild oxen of the world. To date his awards have been many: He has garnered every SCI Grand Slam, and seventy-three of his entries in SCI's record book have placed in the top ten, with four in No. 1 position.

In order to accommodate his immense collection, G. Sequeira had to do a major reconstruction on his trophy room, but he still could not house his 328 different species from five continents. Finally he built two more rooms on his property and filled them with all the Spanish trophies—a total of 1,000 animals, among them 59 gold, 45 silver, and 52 bronze medals, making him, quite possibly, the hunter with the highest number of species in Spain.

G. Sequeira also has a great love for animals, and he protects, breeds, and cares for many red, fallow, and roe deer, mouflon, and wild boar on his property in Spain.

In 1987 he traveled to Australia and New Zealand where in only twenty-one days he was able to collect every species permitted; that same year he also spent twenty days in North America where he traveled to five areas in both countries collecting the last seven animals he lacked from the U.S. and Canada—now totaling forty-three species from North America.

Finally, G. Sequeira has published eight books that detail his adventures spanning the five continents, and is still anxious to increase his collection further—although where he will put the trophies he has no idea!

WILLETT

I am a collector rather than a hunter, though I do have a few trophies that I have shot, such as a whitetail from Brownsville, Texas, and a fourteen-point red deer taken on my farm in Sussex.

I started my collection in 1959 when I became interested in filming deer and wished to acquire examples of British deer. However, when I was offered a collection containing foreign deer trophies, I soon found myself expanding my collection to include African and Asiatic trophies and all wild ungulates.

I was lucky in my collecting to be at the right place and the right time. When owners of large houses either died or moved to smaller premises, many trophies came on the market, and in some cases they were only too delighted to find someone interested in keeping their collections together. Museums too were reassessing their collections, turning out their storerooms and disposing of unwanted specimens. So over the years my collection grew, gaps were filled, and I now have over six hundred specimens on view. Some of the specimens in my collection came from John G. Millais's museum in Norwich and the Sir Edmond Loder collection.

The collection is housed in three converted barns. The first, "African House," is a ninety-foot-long building in which are displayed the African trophies, the smaller of the deer trophies, and some mountain game, such as chamois, tahr, and takin. When I started collecting, I was unable to find museums or collections where one could compare closely related species and subspecies, so I decided to hang my trophies with this in mind. For instance, all the different races of hartebeests are hung together. My three favourite antelope trophies are Hunter hartebeest, bongo, and mountain nyala.

In the "Deer Barn," one can view a full range of Asiatic deer: sika, thamin, hog, and chital, as well as some outstanding sambar and swamp deer (Cervus duvauceli). A selection of British red deer shows the variation found in the antlers of animals from the southwest of England compared to those from Scotland, Europe, Kashmir, and Tibet. I have been told that my display of American wapiti, or elk, is outstanding. Besides the moose, it is interesting to see the variation found in the different races of caribou, from the large mountain or Osborne caribou, through the long round-tined barrens ground type to the shorter flatter heads of the Woodland caribou. Two other interesting exhibits are those of Shomburk deer from Thailand, a species that may have become extinct in the 1930s, and the newly discovered Vietnamese giant muntjac.

The "Sheep Barn" contains an interesting collection of Himalayan sheep, including Marco Polo argali, blue sheep, and urial. The ibex, Siberian, Walia, European, and Sind can be compared, as can the different races of markhor. A selection of both African and Asiatic buffalo can also be viewed.

O'CONNOR

(1902-1978)

Jack O'Connor was one of America's most popular outdoor writers ever. Born on 22 January 1902 in Arizona, he started hunting at an early age. He claimed his first big-game trophy, a mule deer, at the age of 12, beginning what was to be a famous hunting career. He attended universities in both Arizona and Arkansas, the latter from which he graduated in 1925. In 1927 he received an M.A. from the University of Missouri. He met his wife Eleanor in Arkansas, and after graduation they settled in Arizona. In 1934 while he was a professor of journalism at the University of Arizona, he began hunting desert sheep in the Mexican state of Sonora. He started his writing career during the Depression and in 1937 began writing exclusively for Outdoor Life magazine. O'Connor stayed with this publication until his retirement in 1972. He produced 208 bylined articles from 1948 to 1957. In 1973 he was lured out of retirement to write for Petersen's Hunting magazine. He is considered by many to be America's all-time greatest outdoor writer.

O'Connor's long career as a writer started with two novels in the '30s, Conquest and Boomtown. From then on, he wrote well over a dozen books on big-game hunting, rifles, shotguns, as well as another novel, Horse & Buggy West. His hunting experiences stretched over the entire North American continent from the Yukon Territories to Sonora. His first Rocky Mountain ram was taken in 1943 in Alberta, his first Dall sheep in 1945 in the Yukon, his first Stone sheep the following year in British Columbia. He was best known for his love of sheep hunting, of which he took four Grand Slams of American mountain sheep and four Old World species. However, his experiences were by no means limited to this game animal alone. Outside North America, he hunted in Persia, India, and Europe, and made eight safaris to various African countries.

O'Connor was the second recipient of the Weatherby Award, the most prestigious trophy in the big-game hunting world. He was elected to the Hunting Hall of Fame in 1974. A "character" who had strong and vocal opinions on all aspects of hunting and firearms, he died 20 January 1978 while traveling back from Hawaii on the Mariposa, a cruise ship he and Eleanor had taken. Jack and Eleanor, now also dead, left three children.

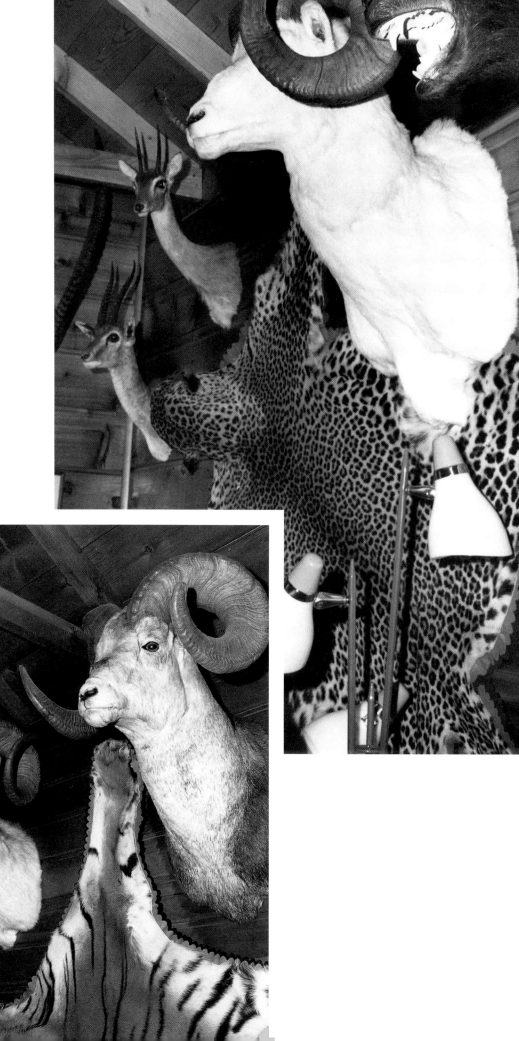

BROCKHOUSE

(1908-1978)

Henry Brockhouse was born in 1908 on a small farm near Edgerton, Minnesota. At a young age his family moved to Sioux Falls where the family operated a grocery store. Being the eldest son, it was Henry's duty to help the family in all capacities. This work ethic made the family grocery and hardware store one of the largest in the state, and in 1978 it was still the most complete hardware store in the United States.

Brockhouse, soft-spoken, well-mannered, and somewhat of an introvert, didn't have many friends because of his commitment to helping with the hardware store. In his spare time he enjoyed hiking along the Big Sioux River. This ignited a burning desire to go pheasant and duck hunting, a desire that was discouraged by his father, who considered it to be a waste of time.

By age nineteen, hunting was Henry's favorite pastime. At the age of twenty-two he married Ethel Palmer and together they had four children. Following the death of his wife, he remarried in 1963 to Bertha Storevik Otten. In the '30s and '40s, Brockhouse hunted local animals, and took his first record elk in Wyoming. In the 1950s Brockhouse hunted in Canada and Alaska; in the 1960s he expanded his hunting to Africa; and during the 1970s he hunted in India, New Zealand, Australia, and Mongolia. Over the years, Brockhouse built up one of the largest private collections of mounted animals in the world. He displayed part of his collection in his Sioux Falls hardware store for many years.

In 1978 Brockhouse passed away, and in 1981 his hardware store closed. The collection was put up for sale. In 1981, the C. J. Delbridge family purchased the collection in its entirety, donating it to the city of Sioux Falls on the condition that a proper building be constructed in which to house it. It was decided that the Delbridge Museum of Natural History would become part of the Great Plains Zoo to enhance the recreational and educational value of both facilities.

The collection was kept in storage until 1984, during which time the "Save the Brockhouse Animals" group was very active in raising the $60,000 necessary to pay Joe Jonas Taxidermy to mount Brockhouse's remaining African elephant, hippo, mountain zebra, Grevy zebra, impala, springbok, and fallow deer. The Delbridge Museum of Natural History opened to the public in 1984.

Approximately 150 mounts are currently on display and are grouped geographically and by habitat. The majority of the mounts are representatives of species from Africa, North America, and Asia. Information and graphics throughout the museum focus on how different animals have adapted to their particular environments, and what their current status is in the wild.

The mounted collection has been placed in natural-looking surroundings called dioramas, which convey a more realistic image of the natural surroundings of different animals, and better highlight the role each species plays in its particular habitat.

GREAT HUNTERS

CABELA

When they started their catalog venture on the kitchen table in 1961, Richard and Mary Cabela had no idea how far-flung their business—or travels—would become. Today, Cabela's, the world's foremost outfitter of hunting, fishing and outdoor gear, does worldwide business, and Dick and Mary's hunting adventures have likewise become global.

From humble single-product 12-fishing-flies-for-a-dollar beginnings, Dick, Mary and Dick's brother Jim built a business that currently features more than 150,000 products offered in more than 60 million catalogs shipped each year to all 50 states and 120 countries.

Like the company, Dick and Mary's hunting adventures began in modest fashion. As the business grew so did their desire to try for some of the most sought-after trophies throughout the world. And while their passports bear stamps from Argentina and Australia to Zambia and Zimbabwe, Dick is quick to name his favorite hunting location: Africa.

On their first trip to Africa, "we really fell in love," Dick said. "Hemingway was right about that. It really gets in your blood."

Unlike the trophies of most hunters, many of Dick and Mary's trophies are viewed by visitors numbering in the hundreds of thousands each year. But then unlike the trophies of most hunters, Dick and Mary's are prominently displayed throughout the three Cabela's catalog showrooms, a 150,000-square-foot store in Owatonna, Minnesota, a 75,000-square-foot store in Sidney, Nebraska, and a 40,000-square-foot store in Kearney, Nebraska.

While not all the hundreds of trophy animals on display in the retail stores can be attributed to Dick and Mary, many of them can. It's a good bet that if it's an African animal, it's probably from one of Dick and Mary's safaris.

In fact, it is the extraordinary collection of animals from throughout the world—in some of the most artistic and realistic settings ever designed—that has helped give Cabela's stores the reputation of providing a shopping experience far and away above any other.

But the animal displays are more than an attention-getter. They are educational and inspiring, and a salute to the sportsmen and women who, as Cabela says, have made it possible for wildlife to flourish. "If it wasn't for hunting, there wouldn't be any animals," he said. "The people who hunt care for the animals far more than the people who don't hunt."

And the Cabelas back that kind of talk with their actions. Dick serves on the national board of directors of the Wildlife Legislative Fund of America and invests his time, money, and effort to protect the hunting, fishing, and trapping heritage of the United States. In addition, the Cabela's corporation annually supports more than 17,000 wildlife and habitat organizations in the United States and Canada and another 100 or more throughout the world.

VITULLO

Born in Argentina, Hugo Vitullo acquired the drive to hunt fifty-two years ago in 1946. First and foremost, Vitullo is a hunter of the grand and exotic South American fauna when this was still legal, including huemul, pampas deer, marsh deer, red brocket deer, brown brocket deer, gray brocket deer, northern pudu, tropical white-tailed deer, and the famous spectacled bear from the Peruvian Andes.

His trophy collection of approximately 1,000 heads includes more than two-hundred specimens of outstanding red deer, making it one of the most important collections for this game animal worldwide. Twenty of his red deer score between 230 and 240 CIC points. Some, including Mr. C. J. McElroy, consider Vitullo's red deer collection to be one of the best ever assembled.

Vitullo's passion for the African fauna has led him to acquire not only the African big four, but also a large variety of antelope, hunted in many safaris over many years. He has also obtained five extraordinary tigers from India and Sumatra.

He is a life member of the Safari Club International. He has received important recognition for his hunting achievements from the club, and he has been honored for his trophies of South America's game animals in SCI's South American awards program. He has qualified for many international award programs.

He has had the honor to entertain hunters such as C. J. McElroy, Hector Cuellar, Donald Cox, Alan and Barbara Sackman, Marcial Gomez Sequeira, and other outstanding SCI and Conseil International de la Chasse members (including its president, Dr. Nicolas Franco) in his home.

WILLIAMS

When we started big-game hunting and fishing, we were two of the few big-game hunters in West Texas. Clayton had hunted game there all his life, and after we built a new office in Ft. Stockton with vaulted ceilings, we decided that we would both go out and harvest some big-game trophies to accent our spacious new office. After reading an article in a hunting magazine about black bear hunting in the northwestern United States, we decided on a trip to Alaska for big game. While there, we were introduced to some sheep hunters, and our obsession began.

The next year, we booked a Dall sheep hunt out of Iliamna, Alaska. It was a beautiful hunt with two sheep trophies, both taken with one shot, that started a thirty-year love affair with chasing sheep all over the world. The challenge of stalking an animal closely and following it through precarious landscape (many times up and over a mountain) is what hunting is about. That's why they call it hunting, and not shooting.

In the first few years, we didn't collect many trophies. Later, however, when we expanded our hunt outside of sheep, and into other countries, our bag grew significantly. We have many marvelous memories: hunting polar bear on dog sleds; chasing Marco Polo sheep in Afghanistan where Clayton challenged our Afghan hunter, Sheik, to a yak race; hunting in Canada on horseback; forging the jungles of Africa; stalking Gobi Desert sheep in Mongolia; and harvesting argali in the high Altai.

Clayton has always been a gentleman and lets me shoot first if we are together. Most of the time, however, we hunt separately, each with a guide, and meet up at night. That's when the competition is all-out fierce!

We are not good tourists, but we have seen much of the world through the "back" door. These trips have been our time together, and when you are in a foreign country, it's nice to have your best friend, hunting companion, and lover—all rolled up into one.

Fifteen years ago, we began an experiment in Texas that created free-range herds of Iranian red sheep and Armenian sheep. The two different herds are thriving in the Davis Mountains of Texas, and each buck qualifies for the Super Slam.

The hunts have been such a big part of our life that we display our memories around us in our living room. Each time we look at an animal, we remember a different person, place, or circumstance that was either pleasant or in some cases not so, but certainly one that is embedded in our minds and in our hearts forever.

Hunting has left us with a lot of good memories, a lifetime of good health, and a heart full of love and gratitude for Mother Nature. Our family of 2 sons, 3 daughters, 2 sons-in-law and 4 grandchildren share our love of hunting and of the great outdoors.

CANTLEY

The Texas trophy room of Kennon and Merilyn Cantley reflects the memories, experiences, and adventures they have garnered from their thirty-four-year worldwide quest for big game—a quest that has taken them from south Texas for whitetail to Asia for Ovis poli and to Africa for the Big Five.

Like many Texas ranch boys, young Kennon came to hunting rather naturally, taking his first deer when he was only five years old. His father, M. K. Cantley, was an avid hunter, but it was Kennon's mother, Betty, who inspired in him his absolute devotion to hunting. From her, Kennon learned the observation skills and patience that have served him so well in his hunting life.

For several years as a very young boy, Kennon kept a nightly diary of fall deer hunts by writing on a sheetrock wall by his bunk in the family's south Texas deer hunting cabin. Later, when the cabin burned, the section of wall containing most of Kennon's diary miraculously survived the fire. In later years, Kennon's parents had the "wall diary" framed and presented to him for Christmas. So meaningful were his boyhood hunting experiences that the diary occupies, to this day, a prominent place in the Cantley trophy room.

For most of his hunting career Kennon, a highly experienced international sheep hunter, has concentrated on mountain species and dangerous game. Merilyn, an accomplished sheep hunter herself, has been at her husband's side for many of these great hunts.

Despite the fact that many of their trophies merit inclusion in various record books, including Boone & Crockett, the Cantleys have steadfastly refused to enter them. Much more important for this Texas couple are the many wonderful friends and friendships from their hunts around the globe that the trophies bring to mind.

Kennon is apprehensive about the direction he feels hunting may be taking. Concerned about the soaring costs of hunting at every level and for all species, he recently stated: "If hunting continues along its current path of elitism, it will soon be beyond the reach of the average working man. If that occurs, hunting as we now know it is doomed for us all. This simply cannot be allowed to happen."

dos Santos

(1929-1997)

Popular Chinese philosophy suggests that a picture is worth a thousand words, but many hunters would say a trophy is worth a thousand pictures! This is the true essence of trophy rooms. The hunter compiles a trophy room as a vivid, everyday reminder of the experiences and emotions from each of his hunting trips.

Mr. Valentim dos Santos was a passionate hunter who was proud of his rifles and hunting equipment, and who enjoyed the memories of his hunts and the trophies that he collected with skilled enthusiasm. He was a formula man, a man who was meticulously organized and loved to manage things. His trophy rooms, containing around 500 trophies, are organized by geographic areas: Africa, America, Asia, etc., each with its native fauna and characteristics.

Mr. Santos took pride in giving his trophies their natural characteristics, such as the "playing" attitude of the apes, the mastodontic nobleness of the elephant, the might of the buffalo, the cold stare in the eyes of the felines, mixed with the majesty of the lion and the wit of the leopard! Being a dedicated hunter, he was conscious of every detail in preserving these treasures of nature.

I remember the love with which Mr. Santos talked about his "cat" collection, always referring to them affectionately. His hunting philosophy was that of an authentic hunter whose desire was to leave a collection of trophy animals to his country as a scientific and cultural display—one that could be enjoyed by future generations.

TODD

For me, my trophy room is a constant reminder of the good hunts I've made with my friends in some of the most beautiful places on earth. When I sit among the heads, horns, and tusks I am surrounded by personal stories. I can feel the African sun as I close in on an elephant bull with Rob Style; hear the crunch of hooves on frosty leaves while hunting Ontario whitetails with Tony Rinomato; and see the dust rise above the grass while hunting Cape buffalo with Ted Gorsline. I've hunted more with these men than with anyone else. They are all my very good friends.

I also have a rack of good and well-used rifles to complement the trophies, and they too evoke memories. I can pick up my Holland and Holland Royal double rifle, maybe the best-made rifle in the world, and remember the day in Zambia with Bryan Findlay-Cooper when we were after a wounded buffalo. On that day I could not close this almost perfect rifle because of a single grass seed on the face! Then there is the fine Kako 375 H&H that I cherish because I have shot most of my Cape buffalo and elephants with it. There is a newer Winchester model 70 in 416 Remington that has proven to be even more effective on buffalo.

In the next room is a mounted lion, and a sixty-pound elephant at the fireplace. There are also some puny cow tusks that still have the power to scare me. They come from a cow who died from a brain shot while in full charge. Her momentum was such that when she hit the ground her tusk went right through her trunk. I have the pictures to prove it.

There's a small grizzly bear rug too. It's true it won't make any book, but so what. It scared me half to death because I was sitting all alone by Old Woman Lake in northern British Columbia when I heard the bear coming up behind me. I fired when it was just a few feet away. I am not sure if the bear even knew that I was there, but I had a grizzly license, and I didn't get hurt so . . . all's well that ends well. And I got that 54-inch Canada moose from the exact same spot where I shot the bear. Talk about lucky spots.

I also have a whole collection of South African trophies from a trip I made there many years ago with Rob Deane. In fact, every head, every tusk, every bit of bone in this trophy room is attached to wonderful memories of the hunt. They all have a story to tell and that is far more important to me than their ranking in any record book. That is what I like the most about my trophy room: It is full of tangible memories, things I can see, and touch, and feel, that remind me of some of the best days of my life.

RIEGER

Wulf Rieger was born on 26 February 1947. As a fourth generation hunter, his passion for nature and the sporting tradition was instilled in him by his father, Franz Rieger (a well-known roe-deer expert in the Baden Württemberg area). It was this tradition that became the foundation of Wulf's love of nature and its fauna.

From the early age of five Wulf went stalking with his father. As he grew older, he developed an urge to venture into unknown areas, and thus he "discovered" the European countries of Austria, Spain, Hungary, Czechoslovakia, and Yugoslavia. Later, venturing beyond the "old" continent, he traveled to Canada and Tanzania. Wulf organized many of his hunts without the assistance of a professional hunter, which brought him into close contact with many village locals who educated him on their traditions. In the early days of his hunting career, Wulf traveled to picturesque hunting regions that were still unspoiled such as Chad, Gabon, Cameroon, Mozambique, Botswana, Ethiopia, and the Central African Republic, always seeking a trail that was not worn out.

He also hunted in Asia, North America (Alaska, in particular), Newfoundland, the Yukon, Mongolia, Dagestan, Siberia, Kazakhstan, Indonesia, Australia, and Nepal, for many unusual animals such as banteng, muntjac, bezoar, and tur.

This German hunter was never interested in a big bag, but rather quality trophies. Foremost he wanted to experience nature in a profoundly close way. His crowning experience was when he hunted elephant in the rain forest with Pygmies in territory that was unknown to them. He also deeply values the memories of his treks in the Himalayas where he camped at 5,000 meters and saw the majestic moon-lit peaks of the highest mountains in the world.

In Wulf Rieger's trophy room you will find record-class bongo, mountain nyala, sitatunga, giant forest hog, and yellow-backed duiker from Africa, and some of the biggest tahr and argali ever recorded from the highlands of Asia. To make the collection complete, he has a library of around 10,000 volumes on hunting and travel, and a fine collection of English double rifles.

SULAK
(1902-1989)

Tony Sulak's parents emigrated from Czechoslovakia in the late 1800s to Chicago, Illinois; from there they moved to a fruit orchard in McMinnville, Oregon. When Tony and his siblings lost their parents, they had a difficult time making ends meet, forcing Tony to learn the task of survival at an early age. As a young man, Tony served in the Marine Corps in WW I where he was introduced to airplanes and developed a passion for them that would last a lifetime.

Tony became an accomplished pilot, obtained a multi-engine rating, and owned and piloted several aircraft throughout the years. After his tour of duty was over, Tony married; he and Gladys moved to Seattle, Washington, and they had two children, Antoinette and Sonia. A few years later, he founded Sulak Manufacturing Company. Tony had taken up hunting, and often went to Canada where he always had good luck bagging grizzly, moose, elk, goat, black bear, mountain lion, and sheep.

Tony's first safari to Africa was in 1960. He enjoyed many fine trips to different countries in Africa, as well as India and Afghanistan. Tony bagged many beautiful trophies throughout the years. He displayed his first trophies in his office at Sulak Manufacturing Company; then, as more were acquired, he moved them to his home. Eventually, Tony purchased a new home, on two acres, in Edmonds, Washington, and built a 30- by 60-foot trophy room. The new house and trophy room provided the Sulaks with 9,000 square feet to house Tony's trophies and to accommodate guests for meetings and parties.

Gladys was a nonhunter, but served as hostess to the hundreds of guests who toured their trophy room. Filled with fine pieces of carved ebony, native spears, masks, shields, bronzes, musical instruments, and wildlife oil paintings, Tony's collections have been enjoyed by school children, senior citizen groups, and the Boy and Girl Scouts. He especially enjoyed watching the school children who came for their yearly field trips.

In 1975, Tony and a few fellow hunters founded the Northwest Chapter of the Safari Club International. The Sulaks hosted Safari Club meetings and dinners for many years, with a typical attendance of sixty to seventy guests.

Tony also had another association with animals—he owned an island filled with six-hundred sheep. He would fly his plane to the eight-hundred-acre farm he called Spieden Island, in the San Juan Islands, near the Canadian border, to supervise the shearing of the sheep. He then marketed the wool, and also recorded the births of new spring lambs. Next to hunting, Tony's Spieden Island, which he owned for thirty years, was a major love.

When Tony became ill with diabetes, he was forced to give up flying, and soon after, he also had to give up hunting. He was never able to finish his list of special animals for his trophy room, but he had a lifetime of living his dream.

GATES
(1922-1988)

The late Elgin T. Gates was born on 6 November 1922 in Salt Creek, Wyoming. He was a hunter from early childhood, starting his hunting career in his home state of Wyoming and later moving to Colorado. Elgin won numerous target shooting awards as a youth. After WW II he settled in Needles, California, where he opened the Needles Trading Post and was one of the founders of the famous California Colorado River Marathon boat race. He moved to Seattle in 1950, continued with his boat racing, and then moved to Newport Beach, California, where he was the West Coast distributor for Mercury boat engines.

Along with his boat racing, he was also a legend in the field of international big game. He hunted the Himalayas of Asia and the plains of East Africa extensively, starting right after WW II. He won the Weatherby Award in 1960, which is considered the Oscar of the hunting world. Gates searched for the unusual and exotic species of big game in far-flung corners of the globe. He pioneered and opened up new hunting areas, blazing trails for others to follow.

It was Elgin Gates and his long time friend Herb Klein who embodied the rise of the modern trophy hunter after WW II. In a vote by an international jury in 1963 to choose the six greatest living hunters in the world, he was selected with this comment: "Elgin Gates is considered by many authorities to be the greatest hunter of them all."

He has 121 African trophies listed in Rowland Ward's Records of Big Game. Together with 43 ranking specimens from Asia and others from North America, his grand total of record-class trophies exceeds 200, an achievement unique in the hunting world for his era.

Gates sold his house in Newport Beach to John Wayne in May of 1965, who converted Gates's 1,400-square-foot trophy room into a private theater. Gates donated his collection of trophies to the Omaha Museum of Natural History where "The Gates Collection" is enjoyed by both the general public and scientists. Gates moved back to Needles, California, and pursued his keen love of archeology and pioneer history by following in the footsteps of the pioneers who crossed the plains; thereafter he moved to Idaho.

Gates was also honored for his lifetime achievements and contributions to the shooting world by being awarded the very prestigious Outstanding American Handgunner Award in 1987.

At the time of his death in November 1988 at age sixty-six, he was a member of the Shikar-Safari Club, the Conseil International de la Chasse, the Camp Fire Club of America, and the Professional Hunter's Association of East Africa. He also was a founder and first president of the International Handgun Metallic Silhouette Association, a position he filled until his death.

ACKNOWLEDGMENT OF PHOTOGRAPHERS

Dort & Meredith Bigg / Gini Haines

Captain John Brandt / George Casias of Creative Images

Henry Brockhouse / Doug Lee of Lawrence & Schiller

Richard & Mary Cabela / Cabela's, Inc.

Carlo Caldesi / Paolo Massini

Kennon & Merilyn Cantley / Illusions

Frank Carlisi / Stephen Lee

Tillman Cavert / Darien Caughorn

Valentim dos Santos / Fotografia Real, Lda.

Doug & Patty Dreeszen / Daniel Tilton of Photographic Solutions

Peter Flack / Brian Farrell

Elgin Gates / Don Bush & Wynn Bullock

Alberto Gutiérrez / Anthony Richardson

Erwin Himmelseher / Peter Strobel Photodesign

Sam Jaksick / Chris Talbot & John Thomas

Larry Kelly / Michael P. Robinson of Robinson's Photography

Robert & Marion Logan / Colin Michie of Photo Visions

Renato Luca / Walesky

Maharajahs / Anne Garde

John Malloy / Harry Jordan

Wayne Pocius / John Kellar Associates Photography Studio

Alan & Barbara Sackman / Phillip Nilsson of Nilsson Photography

Manfred Schröder / Stephan Schütze

Juan Renedo Sedano / SANTI

Marcial G. Sequeira / Juan Roig of Copyright

Huck Spaulding / Bill Demichele

Hubert Thummler / Pablo Oseguera Iturbide

Harry Todd / Chris Barnes Photography

Russell Underdahl / Brett Gordon of Fine Arts

Bernard Van Doren / Nicolas RIOUX DIT BUISSON

Hugo Vitullo / Fotos Thuman

Kenneth Whitehead / Studio Twelve Photography

John Willett / David Grant

Clayton & Modesta Williams / Hendershot

Jesús & Pita Yurén / Anthony Richardson

ACKNOWLEDGMENT for CONTRIBUTORS

Henry Brockhouse / Edward Asper

Richard & Mary Cabela / Joe Arteburn

Kennon Cantley / Robert Anderson

Elgin Gates / Robert Gates

Valentim dos Santos / José Pardal

Herb Klein / Robert Anderson and Alex Barker

Dan Maddox / Tommye Maddox Working

Major Powell-Cotton / Malcom Harmon

Tony Sulak / Sonia Sulak Rathbone

Harry Touby / Kathy Touby Woodward